Wild Ride!

THREE JOURNEYS DOWN THE RODEO ROAD

DAVID A. POULSEN

BALMUR BOOK PUBLISHING

Published in 2000 by Balmur Book Publishing
35 Alvin Avenue, Toronto, Ontario, Canada M4T 2A7

Distributed in Canada by:
General Distribution Services Ltd.
325 Humber College Blvd., Toronto, Ontario M9W 7C3
Tel. (416) 213-1919   Fax (416) 213-1917
Email cservice@genpub.com

Distributed in the United States by:
General Distribution Services Inc.
PMB 128, 4500 Witmer Industrial Estates, Niagara Falls, New York 14305-1386
Toll-free Tel. 1-800-805-1083   Toll-free Fax 1-800-481-6207
Email gdsinc@genpub.com

04   03   02   01   00   1   2   3   4   5

Canadian Cataloguing in Publication Data

Poulsen, David A., 1946–
Wild ride!: three journeys down the rodeo road
ISBN 1-894454-02-2 (bound)
ISBN 1-894454-09-X (pbk.)

1. Rodeos — Canada. 2. Calgary Stampede. 3. Canadian Finals Rodeo. 4. Rodeos — Wyoming — Cheyenne. I. Title.
GV1834.56.C2P68 2000   791.8'4'0971   C00-931912-3

U.S. Cataloging-in-Publication Data
(Library of Congress Standards)

Poulsen, David A.
Wild ride! : three journeys down the rodeo road / David A. Poulsen. — 1st ed.
[240] p.: ill.; cm.
ISBN 1-894454-02-2 (bound)
ISBN 1-894454-09-X (pbk.)

1. Rodeo performers. 2. Wilson, Monica. 3. Armstrong, Kelly. 4. Daines, Duane. I. Title.
791.8/4/092   B   21   2000   CIP

Jacket design: ArtPlus Limited
Text design: ArtPlus Limited

THE CANADA COUNCIL | LE CONSEIL DES ARTS
FOR THE ARTS | DU CANADA
SINCE 1957 | DEPUIS 1957

We acknowledge for their financial support of our publishing program the Canada Council, the Ontario Arts Council, and the Government of Canada through the Book Publishing Industry Development Program (BPIDP).

Printed and bound in Canada

*

*To Barb who kept smiling and kept me
smiling too. — D.A.P.*

To my family in and out of the rodeo arena. — M.W.

*To my heroes: the Keeleys, the Sluggetts, and the Blondins, Glen,
Lari, and Steve, who proved that the thrill of the ride is truly
worth the risk of the fall. To my wife, Robyn, and my family —
thanks will never be enough. To Grandpa Bert and Grandma
Martha. And to everyone else who has enjoyed this incredible
journey with me. — K.A.*

*To Cheryl, all my family and friends in and out of rodeo who
have been with me through it all. — D.D.*

*

*In memory of
Glen Keeley
1970 – 2000*

CONTENTS

✳

ACKNOWLEDGEMENTS

There are a number of people who have made this book possible either by contributing directly to its writing or by carrying the ball for me in some of the things I put aside to research, interview and write. They include Robyn Armstrong, Biff Balcom and Garfield Hockley (heads of Ranch Security at Kelly's place), Austin Beasley, Christina Burrows, the Canadian Professional Rodeo Association, Cheryl Daines, Audrey Daines, Jack Daines, Alysa Fisher, Arnold Gosewich, Ron Getty, Charlie Gray, Roger Lacasse, Rory Lemmel, Project READ-Claresholm, the Professional Rodeo Cowboys Association, Shellee Shaw, Dan Sullivan, Bill Tidball, Gloria Wavrecan, Bob Wilson, the Calgary Exhibition and Stampede and the Appaloosa Horse Club of Canada.

P R O L O G U E

"In every little kid there's a cowboy and in every cowboy,

there's a little kid."

The words are those of Brian Claypool, Canadian Champion Rodeo cowboy, spoken before he and three fellow competitors died in a plane crash in 1979 while en route to a rodeo in the western United States. What he said is as true today as it was then.

The cowboy is still the most imitated individual in our society. While many of us admire firefighters, law enforcement officers and astronauts, few of us don the garb of those heroes as we go about our daily routine. Yet, from the sidewalks of London, New York and Vancouver to the boardrooms of Toronto and Los Angeles, it is not unusual to see men and women in cowboy boots, Wrangler jeans and even the occasional Stetson. There is something about the western way of life and cowboys, from Roy Rogers to seven-time World All-Around Rodeo Champion Ty Murray, that captures our hearts and fires our imaginations.

A lot of what intrigues us has to do with the lifestyle itself, or at least what we perceive that lifestyle to be. Music, literature, television and movies have done much to shape that perception by creating the myth of the free-spirited cowboy and his faithful horse riding over grass-covered hills in search of a stray calf or to rescue a helpless rancher's daughter from the villainous ways of black-hatted bad guys. And while it isn't that way (and probably never was), we don't care since it's the *idea* that takes hold of us.

A few elements of the western way of life still do exist in selected places. Some of the most popular tourist destinations today are the vacation ranches that dot the western United States and Canada. People from North American cities and foreign shores alike reserve their places months in advance to ensure that they will have the opportunity to "ride over wide-open country that I love" and "straddle my old saddle underneath the western sky." For them, the lyrics of the old song represent more than just an escape from the stresses of their everyday lives. For a few glorious days, each of them will have the chance to let that little kid escape — to ride and rope and whoop and holler. And the old west lives again.

But where did this fascination with the west come from? And why is it so compelling? To find the answers we have to travel back in time . . . to the days of the open range and the fledgling cattle industry.

The opening of the American west and, to a lesser extent, the Canadian west was linked to the movement of cattle. It was Christopher Columbus who introduced "beeves" to the New World on his second voyage of exploration in 1493. In the centuries following, through the efforts of Spanish missionaries and their well-trained *vaqueros* ("mounted workers with cows"), the cattle were moved northward through Mexico and eventually into Texas. A century after their arrival in Texas, cattle outnumbered two-legged Texans by six to one.

As the American War between the States ground to its blood-soaked conclusion, Civil War-ravaged Texans returned home to a land that was in economic tatters. The single asset that could be turned into much-needed cash was the thousands of Longhorn cattle that were everywhere, many of them running free and unbranded. The industrialized east wanted beef. In New York City the price of sirloin was an astronomical twenty-five to thirty cents a pound. Texans seized the opportunity.

What followed was a massive roundup and northward movement that over the next twenty years would involve millions of Texas Longhorn cattle. Most of the cattle were driven to the Kansas railheads to be shipped east. But some went to the open ranges of Wyoming, Colorado, Nebraska, Montana and eventually to the western provinces of Canada to provide seed stock for the ranches that were springing up in the lush and seemingly endless prairie grasslands.

There is no doubt that the cattle drives were both thrilling and downright dangerous. Mud, lightning, floods, storms and swollen rivers exacted a terrible toll from both livestock and cowboys. Indians, while peaceable for the most part, often demanded cows as payment for the grass consumed by the herds. More dangerous were the Kansas Jayhawkers, settler-outlaws who had sympathized with the North and had little use for what they regarded as Southern trespassers. The cowboys who rode the trails were indeed brave men. In the decades after, survivors of the drives told their stories — no doubt with appropriate embellishments — to anyone who would listen.

It's not surprising then that we still remember so many of the names of places and people linked with that time. The Chisholm Trail (a depression four football fields wide, the result of millions of hooves that trod those miles, is still in evidence), the railhead towns of Abilene and Dodge City, men like Charles Goodnight and Oliver Loving (their story inspired Larry McMurtry's *Lonesome Dove*) and Wild Bill Hickok — all became famous in part because of their associations with the great cattle drives.

As long as there have been cattle and people to tend them, it seems other people have been fascinated with the relationship between the two. Thus the romantic myth of the cowboy was born. It was fuelled by dime-novel writers like Ned Buntline and Colonel Prentiss Ingraham, then artists like Charley Russell and Frederic Remington and eventually the first western novelist, Owen Wister, whose classic *The Virginian* became the prototype for future generations of western writers, including Zane Grey and Louis L'Amour.

Spectacular though the movement of the cattle was, its time was as short-lived as it was dramatic. Farmers, sheepmen and small-scale ranchers began to arrive on the scene, transported west by rail or wagon train. They brought with them barbed wire and used it to close off the open range. And an era came to an end almost as quickly as it had begun. But while the chisel-faced, freedom-loving men on horseback may have ridden into the sunset, they have yet to ride out of our hearts.

The dust of the trail drives was still settling as the first efforts to preserve the memory of that disappearing era began. Circus-like entertainments — the most famous being the Miller Brothers 101 Ranch Show and Buffalo Bill Cody's Wild West Show — travelled North America and Europe. They featured cowboys, the occasional cowgirl, Indians, horses and guns. The staged spectaculars (which usually included cowboy versus Indian battles) showed off the riding, roping and shooting skills that had made the cowboy famous.

Another form of live western entertainment dedicated to the preservation of the western myth was also emerging. It was called rodeo — from the Spanish word *rodear*, meaning to surround or encircle. Ranch contests that had previously been impromptu challenges between the best horse breakers of neighbouring spreads became formalized competitions that brought cowboys together with the best ropers and riders winning prize money. In 1888 in Prescott, Arizona, the first trophy was awarded to a rodeo winner. Some of rodeo's events, like Roping and Bronc Riding, had their roots in ranch work while others, like Steer Riding and later Bull Riding, were added strictly as entertainment. As the wild west shows disappeared, rodeos grew in size and popularity.

In 1897, Cheyenne launched its Frontier Days, Pendleton's Roundup followed in 1910 and in 1912 an entrepreneurial American cowboy named Guy Weadick persuaded four of western Canada's most prominent ranchers and businessmen to back an idea he had. That idea became the Calgary Stampede.

Today the Stampede, known worldwide as "The Greatest Outdoor Show on Earth," attracts more than one million people annually for a frenzied celebration that is part rodeo, part wild west show and part down-home barn dance. But the centrepiece of the Stampede, just as it was in Weadick's day, is the afternoon rodeo performance that attracts the best cowboys and cowgirls in the world competing for over half a million dollars in prize money. The celebration peaks on the final Sunday of competition when the winners of the six featured events — Bareback Riding, Saddle Bronc Riding, Calf Roping, Steer Wrestling, Bull Riding and Barrel Racing each collects a cheque for $50,000.

But for the people of rodeo who travel the thousands of miles each year, the quest is about much more than money. It has as much to do with bragging rights and the chance to lean against the wooden bar in Sheridan, Wyoming or Medicine Hat, Alberta, and show off the buckle that says to the world that on that day, in that town, at that rodeo . . . you were the best.

INTRODUCTION

Three people — each on a journey. It's a journey down a path they love, the path every rodeo athlete follows. And despite recurring danger, small paycheques (smaller than those paid to any other major league athlete) and endless miles down unfamiliar, often unfriendly highways, it's a path that none of the three would deviate from.

In the pages that follow, these three people will tell their stories. They will share with us their lives in and out of the rodeo arena. They will introduce us to their families and friends, and they will talk about the triumphs and tragedies of their lives. When they've finished, those of us to whom rodeo is the stuff of sportscast highlight reels may understand a little better what drives them not only to do what they do, but to want to do it better than anyone else. While most of us shake our heads and say, "Nothing could make me want to do that," we might begin to understand why these three people and hundreds more like them could never want to do anything else.

Monica Wilson is a barrel racer. She competes in one of rodeo's most popular events. Barrel racing is colourful, fast-paced and easy to understand. It has been called good horsemanship at high speed and that's probably an accurate description of what is essentially a horse race. The women who compete in the event are not only talented and fearless riders, they are also remarkably dedicated. That dedication to their craft is such that on those minus twenty Celsius mornings in the Canadian hinterland, they are outside in thermal underwear and ski suits. And before the sun has made its appearance, they have saddled their horses and mounted up, heading out once more to put in the miles necessary to make both of them champions.

Monica Wilson is a champion in and out of the rodeo arena. She has won some of the biggest rodeos in the world. But the British Columbia native is special for more than her barrel-racing exploits. She is one of the most respected individuals in rodeo today. In 1996 she was named winner of the Guy Weadick Award at the Calgary Stampede. The award goes to the person who best exhibits sportsmanship, dedication to the sport and competitive excellence. In 1999 she was again honoured, this time by being named Canadian Professional Rodeo's Cowboy of the Year. Yes, they'll probably have to change the name of the award but you can forgive the political incorrectness. You see, Monica Wilson is the first woman to receive either honour.

Kelly Armstrong was born and raised cowboy. His connection to rodeo dates back to his great-grandfather, George Armstrong, who competed in every event at the first Calgary Stampede. Born in Saskatchewan, Kelly began his career at the tender age of nine years, when he first began competing in the Boys' Steer Riding event. Like a lot of rodeo kids, Kelly had a plan. That plan was corral-fence simple — he would follow the trail blazed by his great-granddad, his grandfather and his father — the rodeo trail.

As soon as he was old enough — actually before he was old enough — Kelly Armstrong began climbing on the backs of 1,500- to 2,000-pound bucking bulls. It quickly became clear to even the most casual observer that this was a special young man with a special talent. While completing a degree at Vernon (Texas) Regional College (on a full rodeo scholarship), Kelly hit the pro ranks. The result was instant and meteoric. He earned a Canadian Finals Rodeo berth in 1995. Two years later he was the season leader in Canada while climbing as high as fifth in the world standings, thus qualifying for both the Canadian and National Finals Rodeos at the tender age of twenty-one.

The next year, 1998, found him in a similar position when late in the season disaster struck. A bull-riding accident left him with a shattered knee, and Kelly was forced to look at the very real possibility that his career might be over. He spent a full year on the mend and though he was told by doctors he had come close to losing his leg, Kelly promised anyone who would listen that he would one day return. And true to his word, after a delay that lasted a year — and felt like ten, Kelly Armstrong was back in the rodeo arena . . . back where he belonged.

Duane Daines is one of rodeo's best-known and best-liked personalities. Like Kelly Armstrong, he started young, coming up through the ranks of Little Britches and Junior rodeos in the Steer Riding event. Then it was on to high school where he too followed an established family tradition by eventually turning his attention to the Saddle Bronc Riding event. (His father, Jack, and uncle Ivan had both been bronc riders.)

Making the jump to pro ranks at nineteen, Duane quickly began to fashion the success that has made him one of the preeminent bronc riders in the world. During the eighties and nineties, he won many of the biggest rodeos in North America, along with the Canadian Saddle Bronc Riding Championship and the $50,000 bonus on the final Sunday of the Calgary Stampede.

He qualified for the Canadian Finals Rodeo thirteen times and the National Finals Rodeo on nine occasions.

A better than average calf-roper, Duane also collected three Canadian All-Around titles and in 1995 received one of rodeo's most prestigious honours when he was named Cowboy of the Year. It was during that year, while still at the top of his game, that Duane Daines's life was changed forever. The bronc he had drawn reared in the chute at Armstrong, British Columbia, slamming him into the metal bars of the chute, breaking his back and leaving him destined for life in a wheelchair. And while he candidly admits it isn't easy, Duane has accepted this new challenge in exactly the same way he faced riding the hundreds of broncs he went up against during his storied career — with courage, dignity and a will to win that has inspired countless people, in and out of rodeo, since the accident.

Life Before Rodeo

There is a perception, I think, that rodeo people are all alike —

that they grow up surrounded only by other rodeo people, become

rednecks at an early age and live a kind of irresponsible, nomadic

and narcissistic existence ever after — kind of like the cowboys in

the country songs. And there are undoubtedly people in rodeo who

fit that description. But like most generalizations, this one doesn't

stand up well under scrutiny. Today's rodeo competitors come

from a variety of backgrounds and from almost every part of this

country and the United States, as well as Australia, New Zealand,

Brazil and elsewhere. They come to rodeo from different

socioeconomic, educational and even linguistic backgrounds.

There is no template for the rodeo cowboy or cowgirl.

✳ **M O N I C A** ✳

I won my first horse in a poker game when I was eight years old. My dad and uncles had bought some quarter horse mares and sat down to play poker to see who got to pick first. They decided my brother and I were old enough to play and I won the first hand. Maybe that was a good omen.

When I look back at my family heritage, I guess it's no big surprise that horses have been so important in my life. My great uncle, Joseph Chambers of Dereham, Ontario, owned the horse that won the Queen's Plate in 1861. My grandfather on my father's side, J.J. Gillis, graduated from McGill University in medicine in 1909. He and my grandmother Gertrude — who had survived the famous Frank Slide — came west. She became a nurse, my grandfather a real country doctor, making his rounds on horseback.

I was born in Kamloops, British Columbia, the fifth generation of my family to be born in B.C. At the time of my birth, my parents were living on a ranch about twenty miles out of Merritt on Coldwater Creek. When I was five years old, my grandparents on my mother's side, along with two uncles and my dad, bought the Empire Valley Ranch. It wasn't a place that could be got to easily. It was more than two hours from the nearest highway. There was a dirt road about ten miles out of Clinton that headed straight west across the Fraser River and eventually reached the famous Gang Ranch, one of B.C.'s oldest and biggest ranches. Our place bordered the Gang Ranch. I guess it's fair to say that some of my best and worst memories come from those days on the Empire Valley Ranch.

When I was growing up out there in some of the most remote ranch country in British Columbia, rodeo was the farthest thing from my mind. I grew up a ranch girl and for most people then,

ranching and rodeo didn't have much to do with each other. I rod.
lots, pretty well every day in the summer and lots of times all day,
but almost all the riding I did, even as a child, was ranch related.

We ran 2,500 head of cows and 250 horses. Every spring we
had three cattle drives to take cattle to the summer ranges, which
were about one hundred miles from the home ranch. First we
drove the yearling steers, then the heifers, and last to go were the
cows and calves. In the fall we gathered everything and brought
them back to the home ranch.

It was a hard life but that's not how I thought of it. It's just the
way things were. We didn't have power. We had a generator that
my grandfather shut off every night at nine o'clock no matter
what was going on. Breakfast was at six, lunch was at noon and
supper was at six, no exceptions. We had no TV, so our
entertainment was listening to the radio and playing cards. We
played a lot of cards. The phone was another way we amused
ourselves. We were on a party line, and every phone had a speaker
so you could hear anybody who was on the phone. When one of
our neighbours, Shirley Koster, had a baby, her husband, Jack,
went to the phone, cranked the handle once and yelled, "It's a
girl." Everybody for miles knew right then about the Koster baby.

Our lives were never boring. There was always something to
do and there were almost always people around. Because we lived
in some of the best hunting country in North America, my uncles
and my dad acted as guides for a lot of hunters. But it was my
granddad who set the rules. One of his rules was that no one
could shoot anything on the five miles of hay fields coming into
the ranch. He'd get up at three o'clock in the morning and go
down to the hay fields to stand guard over "his" deer. It didn't
matter if the biggest buck in the world was in that hay field,
nobody was allowed to shoot it.

ing a group of guys arrived quite early and asked my
hey could hunt. He said sure, but because it was
breakfast time, he invited them in for breakfast. As we were
sitting down to eat, they introduced themselves. They were Joe
Kapp, Tom Brown, Neil Beaumont and Tom Smith, all from the
B.C. Lions football team. They became regular visitors to the ranch.
They came for duck hunting in the fall, brandings in the spring, and
became good friends of our family. My brother, John, still has the
jersey, number 22, Joe Kapp gave him.

Getting an education in that part of the world wasn't just a
challenge, it was literally worth your life. I remember going to school
for part of one year in a one-room school at the Gang Ranch. But
when the roads got too bad for Mom to drive us the thirty miles to
the school, John, who is one year younger than me, and I stayed
home and took correspondence courses with Mom acting as our
teacher. John and I had different learning styles. My strategy was to
work as hard and as fast as I could so I could get outside and do the
things I liked. John was a more reluctant student and Mom used to
have to pretty well nail him to the chair. It really bugged him that I
was outside while he was still stuck in the house doing school work.

That educational experiment didn't last beyond that one year.
From grade four on, we went to Williams Lake to school. Every
Monday morning, my mother piled us in the car for the two-and-
a-half-hour drive to Williams Lake. Then all of us kids stayed in
Williams Lake for the week. I lived across from the school at a
boarding house called Rosary Hall, which was run by Roman
Catholic nuns. On Friday afternoon, Mom came and got us and
we made the trek back home for the weekend.

I'll never forget some of those trips back and forth to school. At
one point the road took us up and over Dog Creek Mountain, a high,

flat-topped mountain that World War II bombers had used as a landing strip. On one of our journeys — I was ten, I think — a blizzard swept over us just as we reached the top of the mountain. My brother and two sisters — my little sister was just a baby — were in the car with Mom and me. We couldn't see to keep going and in minutes the car was socked in. We tried to dig ourselves out but that was impossible.

I told my mom I'd go for help. Mom knew we had to do something so she let me go. She told me later that as soon as she saw me disappear into that blizzard, she thought letting me out of the car was the craziest thing she'd ever done in her life. It was about eight miles to the nearest farmhouse and I had to use the tops of the fence posts as guides while I walked because that was all I could see. I don't know what I would have done if the snow had got higher than the fence posts before I got to that farmhouse. But I did get there. The farmer hitched up his team to a wagon, went out into the storm and gathered up Mom, my brother and sisters. We were three days in that farmhouse before workmen with D-9 Cats were able to come and plow out the road.

That was probably the scariest but certainly not the only time I walked part of the way to or from school. Just across the Fraser River there was a series of switchbacks at a place the locals called the Coal Pits. There was coal was on both sides of the road at that spot and if it rained hard enough a black sludge slid down and covered the road. When that happened and it happened fairly often, we'd have to stop and walk about twenty miles home.

The Coal Pits were definitely one of the drawbacks to travel out there. My dad was returning home from Vancouver one spring with a thoroughbred stallion he had bought to breed to our quarter horse-mustang type horses. He got to the Coal Pits, couldn't get across, so he decided to unload this half-broke stud horse and ride him home. I guess Dad figured riding twenty miles bareback with just a halter was better than walking. And he was doing all right until about five miles from the house when he came to our band of mares. Things got a little western after that with the mares running up and down the mountains around our place with the stallion right after them and Dad along for the ride, a pretty wild ride at that.

The Coal Pits wasn't a lucky place for my dad. One time he was having a gallstone attack, and my mother was rushing him to hospital. When she got to the coal pits, she saw a vehicle coming from the opposite direction. So she stopped. Unfortunately, she stopped in the middle of the road. That might not have been so bad except that the other vehicle was being driven by another of my uncles and — unbelievably on that road — he had no brakes. So he did what anybody would do in that situation. He crashed into my mom's car.

Some of the workers from the ranch were in the car with my uncle. One was a native fellow who got out of the car and went over to our car where my dad was lying in the back seat pretty sick. He asked what was wrong and when Dad told him he was having a gallstone attack, this guy went up on one of the hills and dug up a couple of plant roots. He told my dad to chew them. Dad did and by the time Mom finally got him to the hospital later that night, Dad was better. So he and Mom turned around and came home.

But there was one place on that road that to me was worse than all the rest. About halfway between Williams Lake and home, the road dropped down to the bottom of Dog Creek Mountain and through the little community of Dog Creek, then started almost immediately up another mountain. About halfway up, a spring flowed over a steep part of the road. It was no big deal in summer but it was awful scary in winter. When it got cold, the water froze over the road. We'd have to get over a patch of ice that sometimes was built up pretty high. There was a steep edge coming off that mountain, and I was sure that one day we were going to slide right over that edge.

So at the bottom of that mountain I would pray — every time. I'd promise God that I'd be *really* good if He'd only let us get over the mountain one more time. Of course, it didn't help my confidence that we were making those trips in a Volkswagen Beetle. I'm not sure it was the right vehicle for that country or that climate but it's what we had. Like most of those cars, it didn't have much of a heater, and I can remember my mom peering through a little defrosted patch of windshield about three inches square while she drove like crazy over those roads.

There were a few times I was glad we had that car. At one spot on the road, just around a sharp corner, there was a new bridge. The old bridge was still there off to the side but it was pretty much rotted through. One day mom missed the turn and we wound up perched (with all four wheels in the air) on one of the remaining crossbeams of the old bridge. That Volkswagen was probably the only vehicle small enough to balance on that beam. And there we sat. If we opened the doors, we could look straight down into the creek below. Driving back the way we came wasn't an option so we eased ourselves out of the car, climbed up and over and slid down the back.

Later an uncle from Prince George and some of his pals came along. They were on their way to the ranch to hunt. We had no idea they were coming but we were awful glad to see them. They'd had a fair amount to drink and enjoyed our predicament a lot more than we did but they did give us a ride back to the ranch.

Maybe that's why I don't have a lot of fear riding horses as fast as they can run. I think after those hair-raising drives to school and back, it probably takes a lot to scare me.

* KELLY *

Life before rodeo? If there was such a thing for me, I think it only lasted a couple of days.

I sometimes think of my life as a journey. And in December of 1997 as I stood on the back of the bucking chutes in the Thomas and Mack Arena in Las Vegas a few seconds before getting on my first bull at the National Finals Rodeo, it was as if I'd finally reached my destination, or at least one of my destinations. But the journey had started almost from the moment my mom brought me into the world.

I was born in Swift Current, Saskatchewan, on August 3, 1976, and my parents had me at some kind of rodeo or gymkhana or horse show when I was three days old. That might be an exaggeration but not much of one.

I definitely come from a rodeo background. My dad, Larry Armstrong, rode all three rough stock events. There wasn't a lot of bull riding back then; they mostly rode cows and steers; bull riding came along some time later. Dad preferred bareback riding and saddle bronc riding, and I think he would have liked for me to get into those events. I did try both but once Dad got a look at my abilities in those events, he quickly realized it would be much safer for me to stick with bull riding.

My grandpa, Bert Armstrong, was a working cowboy. He started working for the Gilchrists on a huge ranch in southeastern Saskatchewan when he was fifteen years old. I remember him telling me that several times he and Grandma Martha spent the winter in a one-room cabin, maybe thirty miles from the ranch headquarters, looking after the Gilchrist cattle. Every morning when Grandpa got up, the first thing he did was fork hay onto a wagon, hitch up the team and head out to feed those cows. In the spring when it was time to sell the yearlings, they trailed them to Maple Creek to put them on the train.

Eventually, years later, he bought his own place at Eastend, Saskatchewan. His rodeo career was like something out of one of those old wild west movies. There would be a rodeo forty or fifty miles away and it was a major social event for everyone in the area. They'd all ride off and spend a week or so competing against the other local hands and partying when the competition stopped.

And if I go still further back, my great-grandpa George (which is my middle name and my dad's as well) came from Colorado in the early 1900s and settled around Magrath, Alberta, for a time before homesteading around Eastend. He rodeoed more than anyone in the family until I came along. He competed at the first Calgary Stampede in 1912.

As a matter of fact, Bill Tidball of the Calgary Stampede did a little digging a few years back and discovered an interesting piece of history about my great-grandpa's life. He went back to the entry sheets from the first Stampede back in 1912 and found out that Great-Grandpa George was entered in all the events at that first Stampede rodeo.

He's also in the National Cowboy Hall of Fame in Oklahoma City. He was the first man to ride the bucking horse Midnight, rode him down in the States somewhere. When I learned that my great-grandpa George wore a blue shirt when he competed at the Calgary Stampede, I decided to continue the tradition.

I guess with that rodeo heritage behind me, it's no big surprise that I went down the same path. It wouldn't have looked very good if I'd become a tennis player or a golf pro. I'd have definitely been going against the grain.

When I was small, my first recollection of home was the place we had on the Frenchman River just outside of Eastend, Saskatchewan. My dad and mom (Bev) ran about 150 black and black brockleface cows. My sisters, Leanne and Wendy — both older than me — were born out there in Saskatchewan. Both of them rodeoed some when they got older, right up until they discovered boys.

My earliest real important memory is that I hated school. In fact, you could say I was a kindergarten dropout. I pretty well had to be surgically removed from my dad's leg so they could take me to kindergarten that first day. It wasn't that I was scared, it was just that I was convinced Dad couldn't possibly run the ranch without me. I kicked up such a fuss that eventually my parents decided it would be easier to let me stay at home. Mom and Dad got some books and started teaching me reading and numbers and things at home. I got a lot of those early fundamentals out on the tractor with Dad. I guess I didn't think riding around on the tractor with him was school exactly, so it was okay.

When I was about five years old, Dad sold the place at Eastend and we ended up on a quarter section just outside of Medicine Hat near the bustling metropolis of Seven Persons. The name pretty well describes the size of the community. There wasn't a lot there but it did have a school. My enthusiasm for getting an education hadn't grown any. Mom and Dad have told me how it took every member of the family to get me on the school bus. My sisters would have to hold my arms so I couldn't grab hold of anything to slow my progress as they dragged me up on the bus. Mom would be right behind us with my book bag and she'd shove a piece of toast in after me as the bus driver was closing the door.

I remember one day in about grade two or three, I made the twenty-mile bus trip to school and as soon as I got there I told the driver I was sick. I managed to convince him that I was at death's door and he drove me back home. Luckily, I made a miraculous recovery just about the time *Mr. Dressup* came on TV later that morning. Mom gave the driver instructions never to bring me home again regardless of the situation.

It wasn't that I couldn't do the work in school; if anything, school was easy for me. But I just didn't want to be there. I was much more comfortable at home in the environment I loved. Like every kid who grows up in the country, I had chores to do. A lot of my chores had to do with feeding the animals, which was what I loved doing most of all. My responsibility for feeding the stock gave me a reason to get out of bed every single day. I guess it was right then I decided raising animals was always going to be a big part of my life.

I'm not one of those people who, as the expression goes, "never makes the same mistake twice." As a kid I was pretty good at making mistakes and I didn't mind repeating a blunder until I really had it mastered. Getting the pickup stuck in the mud and up against a post in the corral was a favourite of mine. There was a bit of a slope to some of the corrals but I was always sure the truck and I could defy the laws of gravity and slippery slop and get back out of there. Unfortunately there were several times we didn't. That particular error in my thinking didn't go down real well with Dad. It was always up to him to get the truck out of the place I had buried it, and I know that at least once I caved in the driver's side door sliding backwards and sideways into a pretty solid post. Another time I tried pulling ahead and took some of the paint off the door of Dad's pickup. I spray-painted it over, which I figured took care of the issue but for some reason Dad was still upset with me. He could be awful unreasonable at times.

"Do you ever think?" was an expression Dad used fairly often during my growing-up days. The problem was I didn't think sometimes . . . or if I did it wasn't about what I was doing, especially if the "doing" was cleaning stalls. Much as I liked working around the animals, I don't think I was ever crazy enough to think that forking manure put any sort of purpose in my life. No, I had already decided there was something else I wanted to devote my life to.

Or maybe there was no decision at all. I can't honestly say there was a time that I didn't know exactly what I was going to do with my life. Riding bulls was a given; it was just always there. When I was in junior high school I had all of my binders covered with bucking bulls' numbers. I knew every bull in Canada — its name, its number and everything it had done in the rodeo arena.

Not that there wasn't the odd speed bump in the road. We had an indoor arena at Medicine Hat — the Circle Three — and there was one bucking chute. Dad put on team ropings every Tuesday night and Saturday, and afterward we'd run something in the bucking chute for me to get on.

I didn't have a proper bull rope to ride with, so I'd just rig something up that I could hang on to. It wasn't long before I started getting pretty cocky. Dad was always pretty careful about what he'd let me ride because he didn't want to spook me and turn me off the sport early. We had this one old roping steer; he was skinny and didn't look like much and damn sure didn't look like he'd buck very hard. One night Dad told me to get on him. I've never been in a worse wreck in my life. That old steer jerked me down, threw me up against the wall and then stepped on my arm. He really did a number on me.

Up to that moment I had been pretty much of a pain in the neck. Every day I'd hound Dad to let me ride something. I'd be at him from first thing in the morning till just about bedtime. But after that steer got the best of me, it was about three weeks before I went knocking on Dad's door. I think the possibility of early retirement from rodeo did cross my mind. But it wasn't long before I had the urge again.

Rodeo wasn't all I did. I did other things and enjoyed them. I played a lot of hockey, for example, when I was growing up. I played right through high school and at a pretty serious level but I wasn't like all those Canadian kids who want to play in the NHL. I knew the direction my life was headed and hockey wasn't it.

I can't say I was ever pushed in the direction of rodeo by my parents or anybody else. Mom and Dad never said this is what you should do or this is what we'd like you to do. It was just something that, once I got into it, was the most natural feeling in the world. Being a cowboy was all there was for me. As far back as I can remember, I was more sure of that than I was of anything else in the world.

✳ **DUANE** ✳

It feels like I've spent most of my life in rings of one kind or another. I pretty much grew up in auction sales rings and rodeo arenas. And I feel real good in both of them.

It was my grandfather, Snowdon Daines, and my grandmother, Ethel, who kind of got things really going for the Daines family here in Alberta. Snowdon wasn't the first Daines in Canada; my family actually goes back four generations in the

Innisfail area. My great-grandparents (Snowdon's parents) came here from England, and their original house is in a historical village in town. The house was a stage stop on the Calgary-Edmonton Trail. My great-grandparents farmed and did some blacksmithing — I guess like most people back then, they did whatever they could to make a living. My great-granddad had draft horses and used them to do a lot of the farm work.

But it was Granddad Snowdon who was the first of the family auctioneers, a tradition that is now in its third generation. Although he didn't rodeo himself, he and my grandmother had seven sons and most of them got into rodeo pretty early on. My dad, Jack, was the second oldest of the boys and he was the little cowboy of the bunch. He dragged four of his younger brothers into rodeo with him.

Jack and his brother, my uncle Ivan, were bronc riders and both of them were successful. Dad won the Novice Bronc Riding Championship of Canada in 1956 and '57, and Ivan was the National Finals Rodeo Champion in 1970.

Rodeo and the auction market were such a big part of my growing-up years, I just thought that was the way all kids were raised. I spent hours with my dad and granddad at the auction market. It was very different back then. The sales were more like farm or ranch sales where everything got sold. Now it's strictly livestock that goes through the ring.

I wasn't much for playing cowboys and Indians as a kid but I do remember Granddad's dog Flicka— he was a big farm dog and us kids used to ride him all day. He'd get sick of us after a while and run under a bush to try to rub us off. I bet there were a lot of days that dog dreaded seeing us cowboy kids busting out of the house ready to ride.

I didn't take rodeo all that seriously in those early years, although I went to rodeos some with my dad. I can remember being at the Calgary Stampede as a little kid and sneaking around, trying to get up close to the page wire fence they used to put up for the bull riding. The chutes were still wooden in those days and the whole thing seemed like something right out of the old west to me. I don't remember any of my dad's rides but I do recall that he'd be announcing a rodeo and at intermission he'd get his chaps on. Right after intermission, he'd come out of the announcer's stand, get on the first bronc and then hustle back up to the microphone to finish the bronc riding and the rest of the rodeo.

In 1960 my dad and some of his brothers built the original rodeo grounds here in Innisfail. It's still the home of the Innisfail Rodeo but the place has changed a lot in the years since. It was there I got my start riding steers, mostly dairy calves. My family ran a Little Britches Rodeo here in Innisfail for over twenty-five years and that's where I got my first taste of actual competition.

Steer riding wasn't at the level back then that it is now. Not many rodeos included it in the program, and it was mostly Little Britches and Junior rodeos that even had the event. Actually, at those Little Britches Rodeos, most of us kids competed in all the events. I even barrel-raced a little, which came in handy later when I married a barrel racer. I'm pretty sure my advice on the subject is invaluable.

I remember when I was nine and had been on a few steers, Dad brought up the idea of me riding at Calgary that summer. He was worried that my mom, Audrey, would hate the idea but Dad was smart. He made sure there were lots of people around when he mentioned it so she couldn't blow up too much. I wouldn't say my dad actually pushed me toward rodeo but he wasn't shy about letting me know which of the sports I was playing was the one that mattered to him.

I took all my schooling in Innisfail, and that's where I got involved with most of the sports I participated in. I also played lead trumpet in the school band, which was something I really enjoyed. Our band director, Keith Mann, was tremendously dedicated and worked our tails off. As a result we were a pretty darn good band. Keith is a very respected musician and has travelled the world. It seems even now there's just nothing he won't do if it's a positive step for the world of music. The level of dedication he displayed was a lesson I was able to put to good use once I started rodeoing at the professional level.

I loved playing football in high school. We played nine-man football, and we weren't real good but we had excellent coaches — those were great years. One of our coaches, Brian Murray, used to run scores at the Calgary Stampede every July. Another coach was our English teacher, and he cut the football players a little slack on the academic side. In my senior year, the team voted me Most Valuable Player, which really meant a lot to me considering I was maybe the skinniest middle linebacker that ever strapped on pads.

During the summers my uncle Danny — who was only a year older than me — and I spent all day every day riding horses. I got to know every square inch of the half section where the rodeo grounds are located. We didn't do much work off horses; we mostly just rode for fun although I did have a quarter horse mare I was trying to break. I didn't get on her often enough, and when I did I didn't ride her right. She bucked me off so often I lost count, although I think five times in one day was the record. I remember spending about an hour trying to catch her one day. By the time I finally did get a halter on her I was so mad, I decided to teach her a lesson. I put my bareback rigging on her and used her for my practice horse that day. About all that accomplished was to make her even harder to catch the next time.

While I was in high school, I worked at the Auction Market after school and in the summer. I really liked working around cattle, something I still enjoy today. But easily the biggest single interest I had as a kid was flying. There was something about airplanes that fascinated me from very early on. I collected pictures of aircraft, especially World War II planes, and my room was full of the models I built. I imagine if I hadn't gone into rodeo I would have made a career of flying, probably commercial aircraft. Eventually my childhood dream of flying did come true although it wasn't airliners I was flying. It was much smaller planes that got me to most of the rodeos I competed at during my career.

By the time I was thirteen or fourteen, I was getting a lot more active in steer riding. More rodeos included the event in their program by that time and I went to a lot of amateur rodeos, mostly Foothills Cowboys Association (FCA) shows. But even then rodeo wasn't a bigger deal to me than any of the other things I was doing. I guess I looked at it as what I did in the summer, just like hockey was what I did in winter.

When I got into high school rodeo, I started riding bareback horses. I went to Dale Trottier's Bareback School, which drove Dad a little nuts because, of course, he thought I should be riding broncs. It was about that time that I got started roping as well. My uncle Franklin was a roper and I was always hanging around, pushing calves and helping out. Danny and I got interested in roping at about the same time. We spent a lot of time learning that part of rodeo and eventually were able to hold our own.

The more I looked around at what was happening in high school rodeo, the more I realized not many guys were staying on in the saddle bronc riding, so I finally decided I better give it a try. I went to my uncle Ivan's school in the spring of 1976, and that got my foot in the door for riding broncs at the high school level. The CBC came around to Ivan's school that year and made a documentary about me as an up-and-coming rodeo kid. It was called *Rodeo Boy*. I remember not liking it too much. They staged some of the stuff, which made it look awful fake to me. In the first scene, they had me looking into the chute with this mean look on my face and saying, serious as hell, "Whatever it takes, I'm gonna be a cowboy." Every time I see that show, I want to gag.

In 1976 at the start of my final year of high school eligibility, I learned there was a high school rodeo All-Around Award. The winner would receive an all-expenses-paid trip to Oklahoma City for the National Finals Rodeo. I figured that would be something pretty neat to shoot for so I decided to work the bareback, saddle bronc and calf roping events to see if I could win it.

I did and that fall I was off to the NFR. When I got down there and saw how great a show it was, it inspired me, no doubt about it. I made a promise to myself that some day I'd be back there as a competitor. I guess when a guy makes that kind of promise to himself, he doesn't even know what it means in terms of how much hard work is involved. But I made the promise anyway, and I'm awful glad I was able to keep it.

When I think about the people who influenced me early on in my life, I'd have to say my dad and my uncles, especially Ivan, Franklin and Danny, were among the people I looked up to. Of course, like all teenagers I went through a time when my parents weren't that cool and that's when I really started to take notice of those uncles of mine. Ivan often came back from the winter rodeos every year with a carful of cowboys, and they'd hang around our place for a while. It was quite a deal for a young kid to have guys like World Champion Bronc Rider Bobby Berger working next to me out in the back pens at the auction market. Not every young guy gets to rub shoulders with some of the top guns of the rodeo world.

In 1978 I won the Canadian Novice Saddle Bronc Riding, and it was then I started to think maybe it was time to really get after the business of riding broncs and roping calves. Although it had been the winter, a year or two before that, when I really started to take note of some of the benefits of a life in rodeo. It was about thirty below for quite a stretch. Ivan was rodeoing down south and sending reports back up to CFAC radio in the afternoons. He'd talk about what was going on at the winter rodeos, what Canadians were winning what, and he'd almost always mention the weather. It seemed like it was eighty degrees Fahrenheit down there just about all the time. I had a job in a sheep-processing plant at the time. Listening to Ivan's reports made me realize I either had to get serious about rodeo or be content with working in a plant and feeding cows in the cold for the rest of my life. It wasn't a difficult choice to make.

2

The Early Years

Like fledglings in every walk of life, there is, for rodeo competitors, a period of adjustment, of learning the ropes and developing the skills needed to succeed. In rodeo, however, where those learning mistakes often result in the body coming in contact with the ground, sometimes at high speed, the growing pains can be much more painful than in other endeavours. It isn't surprising that some quit — what is surprising is that more don't.

* MONICA *

My first exposure to rodeo was at the Williams Lake Stampede, which was (and still is) held over the July 1 weekend. The whole ranch shut down and all of us headed off to town for the big show. And it was a big show, probably the major social event of the year for the entire ranching community. Natives came from all over and set up and stayed for the entire week.

I'd always enjoyed the Stampede but I had no thoughts of wanting to compete or take part at all. But that rodeo turned out to be really important to me for a totally unexpected reason. It was there in 1972 I met a rodeo cowboy named Bob Wilson. I liked him right off but I didn't see him again until the next year when I made a special point of getting back to the Williams Lake Stampede.

I liked him even better then, and Bob and I were married in 1974. I moved to his home in Cardston, Alberta. Living in southern Alberta was a big change for a B.C.-born-and-raised girl but we weren't home all that much. Mostly we travelled to rodeos together — he competed, I watched. Bob qualified for the very first Canadian Finals Rodeo that year in Bull Riding and Steer Wrestling. We were both excited about going to Edmonton for the Finals. I remember that CFR very well because during one of the performances Bob got hung up on a bull. He was being dragged around the arena, and finally Kelly Lacoste, a rodeo clown who happened to be there watching the rodeo, came down out of the stands, jumped into the arena and got Bob free from that bull. Watching my new husband almost get killed wasn't a real positive introduction to the sport of rodeo.

The next year, the Canadian Professional Rodeo Association decided to stage a rodeo in Montreal. By then I was bored with going to rodeos just to watch. When I found out they were short of barrel racers for the rodeo in Montreal, I borrowed a horse from Dee Watt (now Dee Butterfield). She grew up in the Chilcotin, about one hundred miles north of the Empire Valley and went to school with me in Williams Lake. We'd been friends for a long time and Dee had become a top barrel racer.

We headed off to Quebec. I'm not sure if there are many people in professional rodeo who can make the claim that their first pro rodeo took place in Montreal. Although I hadn't spent much time on barrel horses, there was no doubt in my mind that with all the riding I had done in my life, I wouldn't have any trouble.

We arrived in Montreal at about midnight. As we were coming down an off-ramp from the freeway, one of the tires came off our horse trailer and we watched it roll down the hill past us. When we finally caught up with our tire, we stopped at a garage to put it back on and ask directions to the rodeo. We ended up being escorted to the rodeo grounds by a bus, two police cars and about forty people. Though it was now after midnight, as we went through some of the residential areas, people were out on their verandas waving to us. It was like we were a parade, a middle-of-the-night parade.

The rodeo was at a football stadium in Verdun, a suburb of Montreal. The people there were unbelievable. They were so enthusiastic we couldn't warm up our horses before the rodeo. There were thousands of people and they all just wanted to touch the horses. There was one French-Canadian gentleman who followed Bob no matter where he went. He called Bob "Bobbay, Bobbay, Bobbay." He even took all the guys to the wrestling matches. He was typical of the people we met there. They all just loved cowboys and seemed really glad we were there. It was a wonderful experience.

The first night in Verdun, Dee bought a racoon from someone. She kept it in the horse trailer. While we were sitting in the camper later that night, we suddenly heard a bunch of wild screaming coming from the trailer. We ran outside and there was a little fat kid who had somehow got himself wedged in the window of the trailer. He must have wanted to get in there to see the racoon. He couldn't go forward nor could he go back and all he spoke was French. None of us could speak any French but it didn't matter; we had a pretty good idea what he was saying. We knew we had to get the kid out of there. We tried soaping his belly to slide him out but that didn't help. We finally did get him out — a couple of us pulling on his legs and a couple more inside the trailer pushing his head and shoulders — but he was in there for quite a while. He didn't come back to see the racoon again; I guess he lost interest.

I won fourth in the Barrel Racing in Montreal and with that success was wanting to get going on a rodeo career of my own. It couldn't happen right away though. There were family expansion plans right about then that took priority over running barrels.

Randa was born in June of the following year and in August we set out for Utah. Bob was entered in some rodeos down there, and we combined his competing with a little holiday. While we were down there, we stopped at the ranch of Glen and Norma Woods. We knew they had really nice running quarter horses, and we'd decided to see if they had anything for sale that might suit me. The first horse Norma brought out was well over sixteen hands high. His name was Step, short for Stepladder. I took one look and said, "I don't think so. Way too big."

She brought out another horse whose name was Robin. One of Norma's daughters had ridden him in rodeo Queen competitions and had used him for roping and breakaway roping. In fact, they did almost everything on him *but* barrel-race. When we got back home, we used Robin for lots of different things too but along the way I made him into a barrel horse. In October I took him to a rodeo in the hockey rink in Raymond. It was my first rodeo on my own horse and I won third. That was it, I was off and running. I knew rodeo was going to be a big part of my life from that moment on.

I won the Chinook Rodeo Association championship on Robin in 1978. But not long after that he went quite lame. He eventually got some better but wasn't really able to compete at the level I wanted to be at. So I went back to the Woodses' place in Utah, and sure enough, I bought Step. Although he was awfully tall for me, he was really talented and we did quite well together. A Montana barrel racer, Tracy Vaile, tried and tried to buy him from me but I didn't want to let him go. In the meantime I bought another horse — one I called Chicken.

About halfway through that season, I felt I had Chicken running good enough that I could sell Step to Tracy. I did but unfortunately later that fall, Step broke his leg at Raymond at a jackpot. I was there that night and helped Tracy get him to the vet. Tracy was told the leg was totally shattered and that nothing could be done for him. Before Tracy would agree to have the horse put down, she insisted on calling her stepmother in Montana. Her stepmother said there was no way Step was going to be put down and instructed the vet to put magnets and a cast on the injured leg. The vet did that, and unbelievably Step eventually recovered. He was such a wonderful horse. All of us were sick when it looked like he'd have to be put down, and when he came back there were a lot of happy barrel racers.

I had several horses over the next while. One was Dan, a palomino I trained and then borrowed from time to time from Jim and Marlene McGuire. The FCA Finals were in Calgary in 1979 and I had qualified for them. I was running Dan and on my first run I was 14.5 seconds, which was a lot slower than I needed to be. The next night I borrowed a whip from Bobby-June Miller and ran a

13.8. That was the first of four 13.8s we ran in succession. The last one was especially memorable. The McGuires came to watch me ride their horse the final night. Before the rodeo Jim McGuire said to me, "You've got this won if you don't hit a barrel." Those are exactly the words no barrel racer wants to hear just as she's getting ready to run!

Dan and I came blowing in there like a hurricane and hit that first barrel about as hard as I've ever hit one. I let go of my horse and reached down with both hands to try to keep the barrel from falling. I wound up carrying it halfway to the second barrel before I set it down. But at least it was standing up. We still ran a 13.8 but the whole rodeo came to a stop while the judges tried to decide whether moving the barrel twenty feet off the marker was okay. They couldn't find a rule that said a barrel racer *couldn't* do that so the time stood and I was the Finals champion.

I desperately wanted to buy Dan but his owners wanted $30,000 for him and that was in the days when five thousand was considered a pretty big price for a barrel horse. I kept trying to tell myself, "I don't need this horse, I'm fine without him" but then I'd get on him and immediately my thinking would change to "I really want this horse." I never did get him bought. Eventually Marci Nugent bought him and almost immediately started winning money on him just about everywhere she went. That nearly killed me because she was riding "my horse."

In the meantime I bought another horse from a girl in Montana. The horse's name was Pearce, and it was lucky for me that I did buy him because later that year Chicken, who had become my number one mount by that time, died. He was only five. I just know he would have been outstanding if he'd lived. In fact, he already was terrific and had helped me qualify for two

Finals, the FCA and the Chinook Rodeo Association that year. Suddenly I had no horse to ride. Several girls called offering to let me use their horses but I decided to see what Pearce could do. The FCA Finals were at Claresholm that year, and Pearce and I won it. He turned out to be another neat horse for me.

I was still concentrating mainly on amateur rodeos at that time although I had a stout little buckskin horse I rode at a few pro rodeos. We won Brandon together and placed at a couple of others. Still, my focus was on amateur-level rodeos, mostly because rodeo was a family thing for us. We had a five-horse trailer. We loaded that trailer every Friday and all four of us — Randa, our son Riley, Bob and me — off we went. Sometimes we'd get to four or five rodeos on one weekend. Those were really good days.

Although competing was my main interest, I was involved in other aspects of rodeo as well. I had served as secretary for some of the B.C. rodeos when I was younger and had also timed at a number of them. Later I served as secretary of the Indian Rodeo Cowboys Association almost the whole time I was competing at amateur rodeos. Between my involvement with the I.R.C.A. and the fun we were having going to rodeos as a family, I had no intention of turning pro in a full-scale way.

But my thinking was about to change. In June of 1989, Bob and I went on a horse-buying trip that would have a major impact on my life. On that trip I rode, fell in love with, and bought a horse in Texas. His name was Dr. Gizmo; I called him Giz.

✴ KELLY ✴

I can't ever remember going to a rodeo just to watch. That might have happened when I was really little but I don't remember it. My first memory of a rodeo is the first one I rode at. In 1984 I took out my card in the Chinook Rodeo Association and that year went to just a few rodeos. The Boys Steer Riding was tough because we were getting on pretty big cows and little bulls a lot of the time. I was small and slight for my age and that whole first year I never rode one for the eight seconds.

Things slowly got better, and in 1986 I started going a lot harder. My parents bought a van for our rodeo journeys and away we went. They paid $24,000 for that van and when they sold it a few years later, they got a thousand dollars for it. Of course, it had over 400,000 kilometres on it. I made the Finals in the CCA Rodeo Association that year and ended up competing against guys who were quite a bit older than me. Shawn Vant, who was sixteen and had already won a Canadian Steer Riding Championship, was one of them. Going up against guys of that calibre turned out to be a really good learning experience.

Then in 1987 I started going to pro rodeos, and I was fortunate enough to make the Canadian Finals in my first year. I bucked off the first four steers I got on at that CFR but ended up winning the last two rounds so I was pretty happy with how I did. I qualified for the CFR three more times after that and was starting to feel I was pretty well unstoppable.

I lost that feeling in a hurry when I tried riding one-handed. Steer riders have the option of riding with one or two hands and I'd always ridden with two. But I thought it would help my preparation for riding bulls later if I got used to riding with one hand. It was during that period that I really started to doubt my ability. It felt awkward and I fell off everything. But I think it was good that I experimented with it. It probably did help in the long run.

Monica and Giz round the second barrel at the 1999 Calgary Stampede. (MIKE COPEMAN)

Monica with the bronze Guy Weadick Award in 1996 — she's the first and only woman ever to win the award. (WILSON FAMILY COLLECTION)

Just another day in the glamorous life of a rodeo cowgirl — Monica at Ponoka in 1998.
(MIKE COPEMAN)

Monica and Giz make a run at the 1998 Calgary Stampede. (MIKE COPEMAN)

Monica on the move at the Canadian Rodeo Finals in 1996. (MIKE COPEMAN)

With Giz injured, Monica twirls the barrels at the 1999 Canadian Finals Rodeo on Ace.
(MIKE COPEMAN)

PREVIOUS SPREAD: Monica and Giz turn the second barrel at the Ponoka Stampede, a July 1st tradition in Canadian rodeo. (MIKE COPEMAN)

The kids in steer riding take what they do very seriously. The life of a steer rider can best be described as being a full-grown man in a little man's body. I was no different. I wanted to win as bad as any of the adult competitors and I was pretty mad when I didn't, probably even madder then than I am now, although I'm still not good at accepting losing. I was certainly disappointed at the time that I never won the Canadian championship. Finishing second, which I did twice, just didn't cut it.

I looked at rodeo then in much the same way I do now. Many of my attitudes haven't changed much at all. I remember thinking that everything was a big deal in steer riding. I studied the stock the same way the big cowboys did, I tried to act the same way they did and when they helped me get on, my attitude was that they were there just to watch me ride. And I notice the kids riding steers today are the same way I was. They're playing the game I played. And a lot of them are darn good at it.

But as serious as we were about our rodeo careers, we also had a lot of kid-style fun. The travel side of rodeo is a little different when it involves people who are too young to drive. There's a van full of kids and a couple of adults getting them to where they need to go. It's like being on a sleepover all summer long.

There was a fair amount of attitude going on when I rode steers and I have to admit some of it was mine. We thought we were the coolest guys in town, a gang of pistol-packin' gangsters. And, of course, with a mindset like that, we weren't above getting into the odd bit of trouble. When I was about thirteen, I travelled a lot with Austin Beasley. [That hasn't changed. Ten years later, the two boyhood pals still go to the majority of rodeos together.] We'd been joined by a new kid, Tyler Martens. Austin and I felt it was our duty, as veterans, to introduce Tyler to some of the finer points of riding steers at the professional level.

We were doing a B.C. run with Tyler's mom, Wendy, and stepdad, Jay Lundy, who has probably packed more steer riders to more rodeos than anyone on the planet. We were entered at Ashcroft for Sunday and got into town the night before. We spent Saturday night in a hotel and the next morning were up and ripping around the halls of this place as only a bunch of kids that age can rip.

I had made an important discovery earlier that morning. While I was in the shower in our room, I noticed there were magnets in the bottom of the shower curtains. I decided right away that I needed to have me some of those magnets. I found that if I made a little hole in the bottom of the shower curtain, I could pop those magnets out of there in no time at all.

When I'd finished showering, I showed the magnets to Austin, who was just as impressed as I was. Later that morning when we were out running the halls, we realized that when the maids cleaned the rooms, they often left the doors to those rooms open. This was too good an opportunity to pass up. We got the magnets out of twenty-nine shower curtains that morning. We got so good at it we timed ourselves at sixteen to eighteen seconds in and out of a room, magnets in hand.

When we got to the rodeo and showed the other steer riders our haul, they thought we were very cool cats. They hung around, worshipping us for quite a while that day. Being the entrepreneurs we were, we even sold some at a buck a pop. Turned not a bad profit as I recall. And that, we thought, was the end of the adventure. We were wrong.

A few days later I came in the house from doing chores and Dad was waiting for me with a look on his face that I didn't like right off. When I got into trouble, Dad was not the person I wanted handing out the discipline. But there he was, looking real perturbed. "Would you like to tell me about those shower curtains in Ashcroft?" he asked me. The funny thing was I'd already forgotten about it. At that age I had the attention span of a grasshopper and the magnets thing had happened a few days before. As far as I was concerned, it was old news. I had already moved on to new adventures.

But as I thought about it, I did remember the incident. To be honest, I really didn't think there'd be a whole lot of fuss about a bunch of magnets. That's when Dad told me that Jay had just called and he'd got a bill from the hotel for $600. I'm pretty sure Dad must have missed all those programs where psychologists say you shouldn't spank your kids 'cause it messes up their self-esteem. My self-esteem got messed up bad that day. But the worst part was that each of us, Austin, me and Tyler, the rookie, had to write a cheque for $200 to pay for twenty-nine new shower curtains for that hotel. And we had to send an apology letter to the hotel.

Then the following weekend we caught hell again when Austin's mom, Cheryl, who hadn't heard about the Great Magnet Caper, finally got wind of what we'd done. It was in the Humpty's in Salmon Arm, parents at one table, kids at the other, when she got the lowdown. And wouldn't you know it — Austin's self-esteem and his backside both took a whuppin' right there in that restaurant. After that incident, all us steer riders had an unwritten rule that shower curtain magnets were damn safe in any place we stayed.

When my steer riding days were over, it was on to high school rodeo. It was there I tried riding bareback horses and some saddle broncs. I was amazed at how fast they were compared to bulls. I just couldn't keep up with them. And even when I did start to figure things out a little bit, it still hurt a lot. Even though I was struggling at the time with my bull riding, it didn't take me long to figure out that riding bulls came a lot more naturally to me than those other two.

I got on my last bareback horse in 1994 at the Alberta High School Finals. That fall I headed off to college in Vernon, Texas, and the rodeo coach, John Mahoney, told me he'd heard I rode bareback. I told him I was retired and hadn't even brought my rigging to college. From that point on it was bulls only.

I was very fortunate to get to college. I had met Tuff Hedeman in 1986 or '87 when I was riding steers. It was at the rodeo at Cloverdale, British Columbia, and there he was, maybe the greatest bull rider there's ever been helping me get on my steer that day. After that I talked to Tuff at a lot of the Canadian rodeos, and in 1989 I went down to stay with him in Texas. He was running a school and I got on a few bulls there. I mostly just hung out and soaked up the atmosphere and watched Tuff. While I was down there, I got to go to the rodeo at Houston, which totally floored me. It was unbelievable to see a rodeo actually taking place in the Astrodome with all those thousands of people and some of the biggest country music stars performing. It was quite an experience for a thirteen-year-old kid.

I qualified for the National High School Finals Rodeo in Gillette, Wyoming, in 1992. I had talked to Tuff about college as I got nearer to wrapping up high school, and he said he'd be happy to speak to his former coach, John Mahoney, at Vernon (Texas) Regional Junior College. He did and I wound up getting a full scholarship.

I spent three years in Vernon and came away with a degree in Farm and Ranch Management. If somebody had told me when I was a kid and hating school that one day I'd have a college degree, I would have suggested they seek counselling. But, as it turned out, I didn't mind college. I took a lot of agriculture courses that interested me, which helped. Courses like algebra, English, history and government were a different story. They didn't command a lot of my attention. And my grades pretty well reflected my attitude toward those classes.

I guess maybe I grew up pretty sheltered from the real world, but I never even saw drugs until I got to college. We were sitting around one night having a few beers and a team roper lit up this pipe. I remember thinking, "Boy, that American tobacco sure stinks." It was a few days later that I found out what he was really smoking. I decided that was it, I wasn't associating with anybody that had anything to do with drugs. It wasn't long before I realized that if I crossed all the people who did drugs off my list of acquaintances, I was going to lead a pretty lonely life at college.

I still see drugs around rodeo. I don't have any desire to try them because I can't imagine anything being better than the natural high of riding a bull at Pendleton or Cheyenne or Calgary. But they are there both in and out of the arena. In that sense I guess we're no better than any of the other sports that are experiencing those problems.

I graduated in the spring of 1997 but from January of '97 to the end of the term, I spent a total of five days on campus. It wasn't that I didn't like the college — in fact, I liked it a lot and enjoyed some success there. I made it to College Finals Rodeo two out of the three years I was in Vernon.

But Austin and I had made up our minds to rodeo hard that year and try to make it to the NFR. Attending classes just didn't figure into the plan. We realized we didn't ride as good as a lot of guys so our strategy was to out-rodeo them. Our thinking was that since we only stayed on half as often as the top bull riders, we better get to twice as many rodeos as they did. A hundred and fifty rodeos later, we were pretty sick of the road — both of us were getting sour and hard to load — but as crazy as it sounded, our strategy actually worked.

* DUANE *

Nineteen seventy-six was a landmark year for me. That was the year I enrolled in my uncle Ivan's Saddle Bronc Riding School and really started to get interested in that event although I was still riding bareback horses from time to time. In fact I still kid [four times Canadian champion] Robin Burwash that he got my bronze champion's sculpture in the Novice Bareback Riding at the Calgary Stampede in 1977. I went into the Finals with a twelve-point lead on him and got bucked off my last horse. Robin got the bronze and I got the heck out of the Bareback Riding event.

The next year I won the Novice Saddle Bronc Riding at Calgary and got my own bronze. That same year I won the Canadian Novice Saddle Bronc Riding Championship and decided it was time to turn pro. I got both my Canadian and Professional Rodeo Cowboys Association (PRCA) cards and three months after I got on my last novice horse I was riding at Denver. That was quite a jump. I remember that night real well — Joe Marvel, the 1978 World Champion, was warming up next to me.

I was scared to death. It turns out I had reason to be. I got bucked off in a hurry and knocked almost unconscious in the process. But all in all I had a pretty good winter. I won some money — close to $6,000, which wasn't bad winnings at that time. As I look back at it now, I realize I could have won a lot more, but inexperience and some rookie mistakes cost me.

One of the highlights of that first pro year was travelling to a number of rodeos with Brian Claypool. We travelled together through most of April and I really thought I was in the big leagues then. There I was going down the road with one of the superstars. One trip in particular stands out in my mind. We met up at the Ranchman's in Calgary and headed out by car to Medford, Oregon. From there we caught a plane to San Francisco, then another car to get us to Globe, Arizona. I hadn't been to places like San Francisco before and it was quite an adventure for a twenty-year-old kid.

Brian was a pilot, and we spent a lot of time talking about airplanes and flying. Eventually I headed back north to hit some Canadian rodeos. A month later Brian was killed when his plane went down while he was on his way to a rodeo in Las Vegas. Three other cowboys — Lee Coleman, Calvin Bunney and Gary Logan — were also in the plane. The plane had been reported missing and the search for those four cowboys was one of the times in rodeo that will always stand out in my mind.

Like a lot of people, I was very involved in the search. People came from everywhere to do what they could. Pilots, a lot of them cowboys, were in the air for hours and hours at a time and there were endless ground searches as well. Nevertheless the search was unsuccessful. The wreckage wasn't found until the first day of hunting season that fall. When a group of hunters spotted something shiny, they went over to check it out. What they found was Brian's plane. The loss of those four guys was a tremendous blow to rodeo and, of course, a terrible tragedy for the families and friends of all of them. I'm still grateful to have had that time to rodeo with Brian in those weeks just prior to his death.

My rookie year, 1979, continued along fairly well until midsummer when I got hurt at Idaho Falls. I knew I was going to be laid up for about six weeks so I decided to dedicate myself to getting my pilot's licence, something I had dreamed about since I was a kid building those model airplanes. Nineteen seventy-eight had been a record year at the auction market, so Dad and his partners decided to buy an airplane. I was able to get my pilot's licence and since I was the only one who knew how to fly, I got to use the market's plane.

I healed up, and with my new means of transportation I was itching to get back on the trail. Except that now I was a rookie bronc rider *and* a rookie pilot. Doug Elving, one of the pilots who had been involved in the search for the downed cowboys, flew with me for that first while. I did the flying but he was right there with me, which was a good thing.

I really wanted to get back on the rodeo trail because I still had a shot at the PRCA Saddle Bronc Rookie of the Year. I was second even after the layoff, but I knew I had to get going to rodeos if I wanted to keep my hopes of winning it alive. I didn't make it though. I ended up second to Charley Atwell, an Arkansas bronc rider.

Looking back on those early years, I think I may have hurried things along a little too fast and that probably hurt me. I was like a pitcher who isn't really ready for the big leagues but gets called up anyway and has to learn to pitch in the majors. Being a brand-new professional cowboy and a brand-new pilot was maybe a little much. I recall being in the chute at Red Lodge, Montana; I was about to nod my head when a gust of wind blew through there. I remembered that I hadn't tied my airplane down and there I was, sitting on my bronc and trying to look over the back of the chutes to make sure the plane hadn't flipped over. I think it's fair to say I wasn't always as focused as I should have been.

It wasn't until 1983 that I finally qualified for the Canadian Finals Rodeo. I had some chances prior to that and certainly believed I should have been there before '83 but it just didn't work out. Part of the reason it took me as long as it did to get to the CFR was that I wasn't staying within my own circuit. I was travelling with Ivan, and we were going to as many rodeos across the line as we were in Canada. Maybe if I'd concentrated more on Canadian rodeos I might have got to the Finals quicker but, on the other hand, I might not have become the rider I eventually was if I hadn't been competing against the best in the world right from my rookie year on.

I was far from a rookie sensation. In fact, I was just the opposite — a late bloomer, pure and simple. That also figured into my not getting to the CFR sooner than I did. It took me longer than some of the other guys to figure out how to win consistently. I got really frustrated in those early years and started to question myself and my ability. Over and over I asked myself what kind of bronc rider was I if I couldn't even make the Canadian Finals.

Yet there was another part of me that honestly believed there would be a coming-out year. I hoped that if I just stayed with it, things would work out. In 1981 and '82 I felt I was getting better and, sure enough, 1983 was the year I'd been waiting for. I qualified for both the Canadian and National Finals Rodeos. I had a pretty good Canadian Finals for a first-timer and considering the quality of the guys I was up against. Mel Coleman was in his prime; Jim Kelts and Tom Bews were on top of their game — I was in tough, no doubt about it. I held my own, though, and was satisfied with that first CFR.

The National Finals Rodeo was a different story. There was no limit on how many rodeos we could go to back then, and I had entered more than 200 rodeos that year and got to something like 150. I'd worked awfully hard — maybe too hard — to get there. Then I developed a bad case of rookie-itis at the Finals. If I thought the competition at the Canadian Finals had been intimidating, at Oklahoma City I was riding against guys like Clint Johnson and Monty (Hawkeye) Henson — they were just so tough. And the toughest of them all was Brad Gjermundson. He won one of his four World Championships that year.

I got slammed real good in the second round and I was hurting after that. Still, I was determined to get on all my horses no matter how sore I was. I figured I'd worked so hard to get there and I didn't know if I'd ever make it back, so there was no way I wasn't getting on all ten of my horses. I did and even won third in one go-round, which was the highlight of my first NFR.

My next year I didn't have any of those sophomore jinx problems. I got back to both Finals and did better at both of them. I remember making a real good ride the last performance of the NFR that year to win second in the round. That felt really good. That was the last year for the Finals in Oklahoma City. We all knew that the next year it was heading for Las Vegas. The word was that Benny Binion, a major casino owner in Las Vegas, had said that no matter what Oklahoma's best offer was, Las Vegas would double it. Sure enough, the next year the NFR was in Vegas and has been there ever since.

In 1985 I had a terrific season but a lousy NFR. I went to the Finals that year in the top three, which put a completely different complexion on the thing. Instead of just hoping to be decent and win some money, I actually had a chance to win the World

Championship. Everybody wants to win it but it's a different deal altogether when you actually have a chance to win it. I'd rodeoed hard all that year, which might have been a mistake. I had the Finals made by midsummer, but instead of easing up a little in the last part of the season I kept going as hard as ever. I didn't ride well in the fall and that carried over into the Finals. I won a little money at the NFR but I sure didn't have the Finals I needed to have to contend for the World title.

Nineteen eighty-six was a mostly forgettable year. I had a horse flip over on me in the chute at Williams Lake on the July 1 weekend. That put me out for the rest of the summer and most of the fall. I won enough to make the Canadian Finals and had an okay CFR but I didn't qualify for Las Vegas that year.

The next year I was healthy again and glad to be back in the groove. That year I won my first All-Around Cowboy title. I'd always had my eye on the All-Around award because I believe that, especially in Canada, it's a pretty prestigious award to win. In the States, the All-Around Champ just has to compete in any two events — and that takes a great cowboy — but up here you have to compete in a timed event and a riding event to win it. I've always believed that the true mark of an All-Around Cowboy is the ability to work both ends of the arena, in other words, a timed event and a riding event.

I'd kept up my calf roping since my Little Britches and high school rodeo days. At most of the Canadian rodeos, I entered both the Calf Roping and the Saddle Bronc Riding, partly to stay eligible for that All-Around title. Because the Bronc Riding was always my priority, I never practised roping the way Larry Robinson and those other great ropers did. They were at it every day where I maybe roped a couple of times a week. Nevertheless, that year I roped well enough to qualify for the All-Around and also made it to the Canadian Finals in the Bronc Riding.

When the week was over, I was the All-Around Champion of Canada. That meant a lot to me. I'd been after it for a long time but I just hadn't got it done. Though there would be other championships later, that first All-Around probably meant as much to me as anything I've won in the rodeo arena.

Nineteen eighty-eight was going along real well until I made a mistake I would never make again. I felt like I was peaking in July, which is when the big rodeos roll around. I'd qualified for the $50,000 Showdown at the Calgary Stampede but instead of just sitting tight, I went to a couple of rodeos in the days I had off before the final Sunday at Calgary. There were some other guys who wanted to go, and since I was the pilot I felt obligated to take them. We went to Saskatoon, which was fine, and then to Sheridan, Wyoming. That was where disaster struck. I had a nothing horse there but when I came off it, I shattered my knee.

That ended my shot at the fifty grand at Calgary and all but ended my season. Even though I was hurt, we had to get back to Calgary so the guys carried me onto the plane. I knew I couldn't handle the rudder pedals but [bronc rider] Kent Cooper said, "Just get 'er up Dewey and I'll handle the pedals." And he did. It was still a long tough trip for me, and it was even tougher knowing that I'd taken myself out of the $50,000 Showdown. In fact, the following Sunday they began the surgery on my knee just about the exact time the Bronc Riding for the big money was starting.

I had made enough to qualify for the Canadian Finals but right up to the week before the CFR I wasn't sure I'd be able to ride. I did, though, and even managed to throw a scare into those guys. It went down to the last day and John Smith beat me out by five points. I won the last go-round, and if John hadn't placed in the round we'd have gone to a ride-off. It was still a nice ending to what was otherwise a disappointing year. But I did learn a valuable lesson. From that point on I always concentrated on winning where I was at and trying to rodeo smarter than I had in the past.

The Magical Mystery Tour

"The mystique of rodeo." It's an expression one hears a lot and not just from the people directly involved. As with most expressions like this one, the words probably hold different meanings for different people. So what are those meanings? Ask most rodeo competitors and they will repeat, almost by rote, another cliché: "It gets in your blood." What does that really mean? What is it about a sport that pays badly, takes people away from their families for long periods of time and will almost certainly, at some time, shed some of that blood, yet can't (apparently) be purged from the system? The easy answer is they love it. But why?

✳ **MONICA** ✳

I'm not sure I know what people mean when they say rodeo gets in your blood. All I know is that a lot of us work all week just to get to the weekend. I suppose that isn't so very different from other people who ski or camp or play slow pitch on weekends. Except that for us rodeo isn't a pleasant pastime, a relaxing way to enjoy some R and R. Rodeo is our passion. It's who and what we are.

And there's another difference. After we've worked all those hours throughout the week to pay for this habit of ours, we have to drive all night to get to the rodeo. And when the weekend is over, we drive all night to get back home so we can start the whole cycle over again.

I've lost track of the times I've driven all Sunday night, got home at five o'clock in the morning, done chores and headed off to work. I try hard to be pretty cheery about it and most of the time the people at work don't know I haven't been to bed yet. Those are the times I think to myself I must be out of my mind. But then off I go and buy another horse so I can do this some more.

This thing is addictive, there's no doubt about it. And yet if somebody told me I couldn't rodeo any more, one part of me would be relieved. There are all those other things in life I could start doing. But the other part of me — the biggest part of me — would feel awful if I had to step away from rodeo. It's like when people grow up and leave their hometowns and all the friends they grew up with, after a while the communications get slower and slower and finally they stop. I'm sure that happens in rodeo too when people leave it. I'm not ready for that yet.

Part of that passion I talked about has to do with how we feel about each other. I know it gets old too when we keep saying that rodeo people are like family but it's true. Even when I don't see someone for weeks or even months (we may not be at the same rodeo on the same day for that long), I follow the papers and the Internet to see how they're doing. And when we do see each other after a long time, it's like going to a family dinner and seeing everybody again.

I think our sense of community really comes out when someone is hurt or in need for some reason. When [pickup man] Bruce and [timer] Iloe Flewelling had their house burn down, they lost not only the house and everything in it, but also all the mementos and awards that meant so much to them. The rodeo community staged an auction that not only raised a tremendous amount of money but had people donating their own most prized possessions so they could help rodeo friends who needed help right then.

I'd miss all of that so much. Besides there are still a number of things I'd like to accomplish in the sport. I'd love for Randa and me to make the Canadian Finals the same year. That's a dream of mine. And I'd give a lot to qualify for the National Finals Rodeo. I've been close twice but both times I ran out of horsepower in July. I just didn't win enough at the big outdoor rodeos to stay in the top fifteen, which is how many girls qualify for the NFR.

It's incredibly difficult to make the NFR. When I see what some of the girls are doing and what kind of money they're spending, I realize it's getting tougher every year. It really isn't a level playing field because of the dollars some people can spend while others have no choice but to train a young horse and hope it works out. Then there's the reality that some of the girls are on the road constantly, living in their trailers and making short — or at least shorter — jaunts to the next place. Others of us have to work at a job and then drive thirty-eight hours to get to San Antone, for instance. But there are still a few NFR spots available to the girls who are on a realistic budget, and one day I'd like to fill one of those spots.

Every one of us wants to win every rodeo we go to but that doesn't stop us from being happy for someone else's success. In all the barrel races I've been in, I don't think I've ever hoped for someone else to lose. I want to make the best run I can make on that day and that's what I concentrate on. Maybe our sport is a little unique in that way; it's not about beating other people. It's about wanting to know how well I can do.

In fact, most of the time I'm thinking so hard about what I want to do, I seldom hear another girl's time when it's announced. Maybe some barrel racers look at it differently, but I really don't think many girls are hoping for someone to hit a barrel. In fact, I think most girls really feel for each other when something bad happens, especially something really bad. When a barrel racer's horse dies, all of us feel the pain, maybe even as much as the person who lost the horse, partly because we know that the same thing can happen to any of us. Anyone who has ever lost a favourite horse knows that it's almost as terrible as losing a loved one.

I've often thought about what I'd be doing if I wasn't in rodeo. I took one year of college at Kamloops College before I was married, and I think if I wasn't doing what I'm doing I'd be some sort of lab technician in a hospital or research laboratory. That side of the medical profession has always interested me. Or I'd have become a teacher. I've always thought I would have enjoyed teaching at about the grade five level. Plus having a job that gives weekends and summers off isn't a bad thing for someone who wants to rodeo and still have a decent livelihood.

There are downsides to rodeo, no doubt about it. For instance, most of us work all week, ride our horses at night and are back on the road almost every weekend. As a result we spend most of our time with other rodeo people, which is good in one way because we really are like family, as I said. But it also means that we all tend to end up thinking the same way and having the same attitudes. I'm not sure that's a good thing. I tend to be an independent thinker, and I sometimes think there aren't enough people who really think for themselves in our sport. It's like there are certain attitudes we're expected to have as cowboys and cowgirls, and I guess a lot of people just find it easier to adopt those attitudes than to be original.

And, of course, there's the danger. Although rodeo is more dangerous than a lot of other sports, it's not something I think about. Because we spend so much time on the road, the travel to and from rodeos is one of the scariest parts of our lives. I try to drive defensively because it's not so much what I do when I'm on the road as what that other person who might be drunk or even more tired than I am might do. I think most rodeo people take their driving very seriously, partly because we have the responsibility for the safety of the other people travelling with us and the horses behind us.

As for danger at the rodeos themselves, I still cringe during the Bull Riding event. I don't know how any mother can let her child grow up to be a bull rider. It's probably because most don't have much say in the matter. I have a lot of sympathy for those moms because if I had a son who rode bulls, I'd dread it every time he entered a rodeo. When Riley was three years old, riding bulls was all he talked about. We'd take him to a rodeo, and when it was over he could tell us what every bull did, which cowboys rode and which ones didn't and what their scores were. He could even describe each rider's style, whether he rode like Donnie Gay or what. His obsession with bull riding just scared the living daylights out of me. The first thing we did was get a rope into his hands and put him on a horse. Thank God, it worked.

The bottom line for me about rodeo is that it's fun. Even if things have gone badly for me in the Barrel Racing, I can usually find something to be happy about. I can look out into that arena and see someone make a good ride in the Bronc Riding or a great run in the dogging and suddenly it's not such a bad day any more. I realize how fortunate I am to be doing something I love to do. One of the easiest ways to remind myself how lucky I am is to go to a hospital and see the kids in the children's wards. I don't do a lot of complaining after that.

But the single thing I love most about this sport is that it doesn't matter how much you messed up today, there's another rodeo to go to tomorrow. I sometimes think about people who train for the Olympics. They work for four years, and then they've got one chance to get it right. They have to win on that day in that stadium and that's it for another four years. I don't think I could do that. I can't imagine training all that time for that one shot and hitting a barrel in that one race.

* KELLY *

I can't imagine life without rodeo. I consider myself so fortunate to be able to earn a living doing something I love. The thought of getting up every day and going to work in a skyscraper in downtown Calgary depresses me. I sometimes wonder if many of the people in the world are happy doing what they're doing. To be honest, I doubt it. How many people walk in the door of the office or the plant they work at and say, "Boy, I'm glad to be at work today." I'm thinking not many. My guess is that for most people life isn't so much enjoying what they're doing as it is tolerating what they're doing. And they have to. Because for most of them, they know that just down the road there's a job that's even worse.

But for me even a bad day is a pretty good one if I'm at a rodeo . . . to the point that sometimes it feels like I'm living a dream. When I arrive at a rodeo and begin to feel the atmosphere and the music starts playing and the announcer starts talking, right away I feel good, my motor gets to running. And because I know I'll be riding a bull at that rodeo a little later on, I feel a sense of anticipation building in me. A rodeo is a magic place for me. I think I'll still have that feeling even after my riding career is over.

Even some of the parts of rodeo that aren't so great, like getting in the truck and driving for twenty or thirty hours, beat the hell out of getting up in the morning and going to a nine-to-five job. If the day ever comes that I wake up in the morning and rodeo isn't the first thing I think about, and when I go to bed at night it isn't the last thing I think about and when I'm asleep it isn't what I'm dreaming about, then I guess that will be the time to think about hanging up the bull rope.

If there's one rodeo that symbolizes why this sport is so special to the people who are in it, I believe it's the National Finals Rodeo. It's the rodeo guys like me dream of competing at from the time we're old enough to know what rodeo is all about. In 1997, Austin and I achieved our goal of getting to the NFR.

Along the way, I qualified for the Canadian Finals as well. I rode all six of my bulls that year and placed in all but one round. In fact, it went down to the last day, and Robert Bowers beat me out for the championship. He rode great all week and deserved to win it. I would have liked to win, but what the heck, I guess second is better than third.

A few weeks later we were in Las Vegas at our first National Finals Rodeo. Along with Mike White, who went on to win the world title in 1999, Austin and I were the youngest guys there. That whole experience was amazing. I'm not sure of the exact meaning of "mystique" but if there's a rodeo in the world that has it, it's the NFR.

The atmosphere there is like no other. The night before the first performance all the contestants received their NFR jackets, and that's when I really started to get a feel for what I'd accomplished. It sounds weird; hell, it's only a coat, but seeing my name on one was one of the proudest moments of my life.

But I think it was during the grand entry the first night that it hit me, that I actually realized I was there. All the contestants ride in on horseback during the NFR Grand Entry and just to look around at the greatest rodeo athletes in the world sitting there on horseback waiting to go in and then to hear the people cheering like I've never heard anywhere was unbelievable. It gave me butterflies every night — those minutes just before the start of the rodeo — but that first night was something I'll never forget. And then suddenly there I was riding in to the Thomas and Mack arena behind the Canadian flag and grinning so hard, my face hurt.

A couple of hours later it was time to ride my first bull of my first NFR. Things didn't seem all that much different in the locker room. I was actually pretty laid back. I got ready and when it was time, I strolled out behind the chutes with the other bull riders. I guess it was about the time they started rolling the bulls in that I experienced another one of those special moments — as I realized

I was standing in the same place I'd watched my heroes stand since I was four or five years old. I remember thinking there might be a kid somewhere in North America sitting at home watching me.

When my turn came, I got down into the chute, warmed up my rope and got set. I thought I was ready, really ready to do something good. I nodded my head and it was over. I don't think I was even finished nodding when my head hit the ground — sort of in mid-nod. My first moment in the NFR spotlight had been a short one. Damn, that bugged me. I'd seen that bull at least twenty times during the regular season and I know if I'd drawn him at Baton Rouge, Louisiana, or Belton, Texas, it would have been no big deal.

But as it turned out, hitting the ground that fast on that first night might have been a good thing. It woke me up — got my feet back on the ground and after that I was ready to take care of business. The next night I had a bull called Slick Willie from the Southern Rodeo Company. I rode him and won the round. What made that special was knowing that the year before, Tuff had won the second round on the same bull. Overall I rode four of the ten bulls I got on and won $33,000 at the '97 NFR. It was okay but nothing special. I'd messed up some pretty good bulls. No excuses, I just didn't do as well as I wanted to and I was disappointed in myself.

One of the hardest questions I've ever been asked is the one I heard so many times after I got hurt at Edmonton in 1998. People asked me, "If this is it, if you're unable to ride again, are you going to be satisfied with what you've done in your career?" I thought about that a lot and I finally realized that if I could never ride again, I would definitely feel like I'd left a lot of unfinished business. Sure, I've won some championships and there are probably people out there who would be more than happy to do in their whole life what I've done before I'm twenty-five, but for me it's not enough.

That injury at the 1998 Canadian Finals did more than wreck one of my legs, it also pulled the rug out from under me. Up to that time my career was going so well it sometimes felt like I'd just go somewhere and they'd pay me. The problem was I was taking the whole thing for granted. Getting hurt and very nearly having rodeo taken away from me forever was definitely a wake-up call. I made up my mind that if I got back riding I'd never again take lightly the opportunity to be a cowboy. Sitting there watching the 1999 National Finals Rodeo on TV, I told a few people that if I could be at the NFR I'd get on the pen of eliminators every night. That's how bad I wanted to be there.

The doctors had told me there was a pretty good chance I wouldn't ride again. In fact, they said I was lucky I didn't lose my leg. When three doctors say that, it definitely gets a guy's attention. As good as riding bulls is, walking around for the rest of my life is better. Not long before he was killed, Glen Keeley and I talked about riding bulls. Glen reminded me that I'm only going to ride bulls for less than a third of my life. It's an important part of my life but it is only one part of it. Hearing Glen say that made me think about some things. That's when I decided to take all the time off I needed before I came back. Now that I am back I'm enjoying it more than I ever did.

I don't think about injury and the danger factor more now than I did before I was hurt. I don't think fear enters into what we do as bull riders. I can't get down on a bull's back in the chute with fear in my mind. There's nerves and there's tension. The heart's pumping for damn sure. But I don't think any of that is actual fear. In fact, I can't imagine any bull rider getting on if he was afraid for even a second. I dealt with the risk factor when I first started riding bulls. And I made my decision. I don't need to lose sleep over it now.

The fat guy that comes out of the stands and wants to get on a bull to impress his girl friend — he's been talking the talk and now he has to walk the walk — that guy's scared shitless and he should be.

I will admit that the first couple of bulls coming back after an injury are a little more nerve-racking than usual because the injury is still fresh in your mind. Austin and I have both been out for long stretches, and we've talked about it. It was tough for both of us coming back. But the anxiety lasted a couple of bulls and it was over with.

What most people don't realize as they're sitting in the stands watching a rodeo is how much preparation goes into every ride. By the time we get on that bull we've prepared ourselves physically — we're in as good shape as any athletes out there — we've got ourselves mentally ready to face the challenge, and we've done our homework. We've talked to guys who have been on the bull before and we've studied him at other rodeos and on TV.

There are so many elements to staying on a bull, and danger is only one of those elements. We're concentrating so hard on all the things we need to do to ride for eight seconds that worrying about getting hurt honestly doesn't enter into our thought process.

We have people in the arena helping us as well. The bullfighters are a very important part of what we do. There's often a lot of communication between the bullfighters and the bull riders. They'll come to us before the ride and say, "Heads up getting off this bull," or "Wait until we've got his attention." Nobody knows the bulls any better than the bullfighters. They have to know every step that bull is likely to take, so we talk to them about what a particular bull might do. [Notice Kelly doesn't call them clowns. There are clowns at rodeos. Sometimes referred to as "barrelmen," they're the guys whose job is to make the spectators laugh. And some of them are tremendous entertainers. But the job of bullfighters is a serious one. They wear clown clothes but their job is cowboy protection. They save lives, and there's nothing clownish about that.]

If I have a fear in rodeo it's the fear of failing. It's the same fear I have of failing at life. I take it personally when I get bucked off. It means I failed plain and simple. I was given a test and I didn't pass. I look at the time I drew Rapid Fire at the NFR. He was the Bull of the Year and he'd had been spectacular all year. That's as nervous as I've ever been before getting on any bull. I'm usually calm and laid back before a ride even when I've drawn one of the real toughs, but I didn't sleep the night before ol' Rapid Fire.

Even then it wasn't the fear of getting hurt so much as it was the fear of being outclassed. I was still sweating in the dressing room in the minutes right before I was supposed to get on him. But once I put my rope on him and sat on the load-up chute as they were running him in, I was all right. I even talked to him. "You red son-of-a-bitch, you aren't any better than me."

And that was true. He'd had to earn the right to be there just like I had. He'd had a good year and I'd had a good year. That made us even. When I finally did get on him I was calm, relaxed and loose. He bucked me off but it wasn't like he intimidated me. I went after him. My attitude was good, I did my best and it was just a case of him being better than me that day.

And it was a good day. I was at the National Finals Rodeo doing what I love. Hell, what could be better than that?

✳ DUANE ✳

What has always made rodeo especially rewarding for me is the challenge. Every day is a new challenge — we challenge ourselves, we challenge the bucking horses — it's a lifestyle that is made up of constantly being put to the test. I like that.

Rodeo gave me the chance to do what I wanted to do, how I wanted to do it. It's certainly not a glamorous life; I think that's one of the big misconceptions. I remember a time early in my career that sums up all that glamour real well. I was in a motel room in some little place in Montana; we'd been to Kalispell and Douglas, Wyoming, already that day and were on our way home. I was lying on the bed watching a football game — me and a bunch of ice bags. I kept moving them to different parts of my body. I had so many aches and pains I didn't have enough ice for all of them. But the weird thing is I felt good about what I'd done that day. It wasn't a feeling of how exciting my life was or how cool it was to be a cowboy so much as it was just a feeling of being happy with where I was and what I was doing.

There's also a feeling of wanting to show all the people who don't think you can do it. I remember a guy saying to me, "Yeah, you're going to all these rodeos but are you actually winning anything?" Right then my attitude became "I'll show you, you son-of-a-gun." So while we do it for ourselves, there's also a part of us that wants to show somebody else what we can do.

Maybe that's the reason I always pushed myself. I know there are people who feel that maybe I pushed a little too hard, that if I'd played it safe a little more often I might have won more. Who knows, maybe they're right, but I always wanted to drive myself as hard as I could. Even in my last year, I was out there wanting to show people I still had it.

I've always been proud to be a cowboy. From the moment I turned professional, I had my cowboy hat on whether it was at a rodeo in Texas or an airport in Atlanta. I always believed that if I looked good, I felt good and if I felt good, I rode good. That's something I think I learned from the top guys in rodeo. That's how they were and I wanted to be like that too — very professional in the way I did things. I guess it had something to do with the mystique of being a cowboy. I'm still that way today.

My heroes in the rodeo world weren't always the guys who won the most. I have a lot of respect for any guy who goes out there and tries his ass off every time. I admire guys who go out there against the odds and make good rides. I remember a few years ago at the Canadian Finals Rodeo there was a guy — Ed Gentles from out in B.C. He rolled into Edmonton with his fingers totally mangled from the canopy of a Cat he'd been running. He didn't say anything about it. I didn't even know he was hurt until the third night of the CFR. He was in so much pain I don't even know how he held onto the rein. But he was out there giving it all he had while some of those other guys, the media darlings, they'd get a little scrape and it was front-page news.

One of the people I admired a tremendous amount was Glen Keeley, who lost his life not long ago in a Bull Riding accident. I think everybody who knew Glen admired him. He was a guy who gave it all he had every time he got on. Plus he had tremendous talent and loved what he was doing. I respected Glen and I think a lot of people did. He's a guy our sport will miss for a long time.

One of the great things about rodeo is the men and women who are in it. They're the kind of people I want to be with. Now that I'm in the (so-called) real world, I meet lots of good, solid-as-a-rock people, but there are also a bunch of whining, crying types. They're the ones I want to tell to "get a life."

I guess I'm lucky that one of the more colourful characters in this business happens to be my dad. I get a kick out of him and as the years go by, I admire more and more what he's done with his life. He has his own style, which is very different from mine, and I think we work well together because of it. He's very outgoing where I'm more of a softer sell. What I like most about him is that he gets the job done. He doesn't just talk about doing something. What he says he's going to do, he does.

I love my dad but he can drive me nuts sometimes too. I guess he wouldn't be Jack if he didn't do that. We talk rodeo just about every day of the year. He's always been tremendously supportive of my rodeo career. He'd fly down to the winter rodeos to watch me whether I was doing well or not.

That often made for some of those "Jack" moments. I'd been competing at Fort Worth for ten or twelve years. Dad decided he better get down there to see me ride. It was his first time to that rodeo but he wasn't there a half hour before he was up in the VIP lounge drinking the committee's whisky and telling stories. And a short time later he had a bunch of cowboys up there too. We'd never been invited up there ever but a little thing like that never stopped Jack.

Another time, while Dad was at the Reno Rodeo, he was visiting with some of his friends from the Gold Coast. Steve Fexer from the Gold Coast stuck a badge on him so once again he could go up to the VIP area. As soon as he got there, everybody was coming up and shaking his hand and it was, "Jack, how ya doin'?" and "Jack, good to see ya." Dad wasn't sure what the deal was or why everybody was all over him. He'd been there the year before but couldn't believe, even as hospitable as Americans are, they'd remember him a year later.

When someone thanked him for bringing the stagecoach to the rodeos, Dad realized he was wearing the badge of Jack Binion, definitely one of the big guns down there. (Binion's Horseshoe Casino takes a stage coach to a number of rodeos.) One thing about Dad, though, he just rolled on with it and had himself a pretty good day as that other Jack.

I guess the thing about him is that he was a cowboy since he was old enough to know there was such a thing. He never really got the chance to rodeo like he would have liked; it was a tough era back in the fifties and sixties and he had to go to work. I think that's one of the reasons he's enjoyed my career so much. He's been behind me every step of the way. If I needed help, I always knew where to get it. Dad wasn't like some of those hockey and figure skating parents, the ones who are just plain embarrassing. He was just there.

My dad is living his dream every day. Along the way he's doing a lot of good things for the sport, from quite probably being the inventor of the Sheep Riding event that has become so popular in recent years to running a rodeo that in its forty-year history has become one of the best in North America. I'm sure that's why he's one of the newest members of the Canadian Rodeo Hall of Fame.

There are special times in our lives and our careers that make us stop and think. One of the most special moments for me takes place every year at the Canadian Finals Rodeo. The dates of the CFR always include Remembrance Day. And one of the things that happens at the Finals is a kind of tribute during the November 11 performance to Remembrance Day and what it stands for.

I've always been interested in history and have always had a tremendous respect for our veterans. That doesn't mean I glorify war at all, but I really do appreciate the sacrifices so many people made during the wars. It really hits home when I'm at the Finals doing exactly what I want to be doing with my life. Part of the reason I have that freedom is that a whole lot of people fought and many of them died to give me and everybody that gift. Every time they have that little ceremony I realize how lucky we are. So often we're at the Finals and worrying about the horse we've drawn or how the judging will go. Then they have that minute of silence for people who were younger than me when they had to leave home and fight for this country. It kind of puts it all in perspective.

Silent Partners

Animals are as vital to the sport of rodeo as cowboys, cowgirls and bucking chutes. In the rough stock (riding) events, cowboys have to make the eight-second horn in order to get paid. Yet the contest between man and animal is far more a partnership than a battle. And, because fifty per cent of the cowboy's score is based on the bucking action of the animal beneath him, there is a surprising feeling of kinship on the part of the man for the animal he is matched up with. For barrel racers, the situation is very different. In rodeo's timed events, including Barrel Racing, contestants, for the most part, ride their own horses. These are horses they have either purchased or raised. Most will have spent thousands of hours training, conditioning, hauling and competing *on those horses. They become friends, almost literally family, and competitors are as attuned to the whims, moods and physical and emotional needs of their horses as they are to those of their children. Stock contractors and those who raise bucking animals for rodeo display that same degree of caring. It's a part of the sport that is not understood and, in fact, is often misunderstood.*

❋ MONICA ❋

Rodeo wouldn't be rodeo without the animals that are such a big part of what we do. Every event involves animals in one way or another and I believe it's the animals that attract most competitors (and most fans) to rodeo. I think all of us in this sport love the animals that we compete on or (in the riding events) against.

When I win I think I'm as happy for my horse as I am for me. Whenever you talk to a barrel racer after a good run, she's spending most of her time talking about how great her horse was during the run. That's because whether we're riding horses that run fast or we're trying to ride horses and bulls that want to buck us off or we own that bucking stock — all of us honestly admire these animals that give us so much.

Not long ago I sat down and watched the $50,000 round from the '98 Stampede on video. I slowed it down so I could watch Kristie Peterson and Bozo make their championship run in super-slow motion. I couldn't believe how beautiful it was. It's hard to comprehend how a horse can be that good. Watching that run over and over, I actually cried. I sent Kristie a letter to tell her it was the greatest thing I'd seen in a long time.

I don't think I'm unique in feeling that way. I've seen rough, tough cowboys break down over the loss of a horse. Rough stock cowboys often tip their hat to a horse that has thrown them off. They're acknowledging that on that day the horse was better.

I've been lucky to have had some very good horses in my career but the best one I've ever owned is Dr. Gizmo. I met him during that horse-buying expedition to Oklahoma and Texas in 1989. I tried out maybe ten horses. I rode Giz in a huge pen at Stephenville, Texas, and just loped him around the very outside of the pen. He was a skinny little nothing-special-looking horse but when I rode him, he just floated. Bob was standing in one corner and as I went by him I said, "I want him."

I paid $7,500 for him, and the next day we stopped at an arena in Colorado that was owned by some friends of ours. I was so excited about my new horse that we went to their barrel patch so I could show off what Giz could do. He ran away with me. He hadn't shown any signs of that the day before at all. I don't know if he'd been drugged or what when I tried him out, but he was a very different horse in Colorado. That's why I advise girls to be so careful when they're buying horses, especially from someone they don't know.

The first rodeo I ran him at in Canada, he went down the wall with me. What that means is that he didn't turn the first barrel but just kept running to the other end of the arena. He did that regularly at first. For a while I thought it was me — that there was something I was doing to trigger him running off. But I came to realize it wasn't me at all. He already had that in him when I bought him. He could run faster than anything I've ever been on in my life but he was scared to death. It was a long, slow process to fix him.

When he was five years old, we were still having some problems. I decided to phone Beatrice Lydecker, an animal psychic, down in the States. She asked me what kind of animal I was inquiring about. When I told her it was a horse named Dr. Gizmo, she said, "Oh, my goodness, we have a fiery little horse here, don't we? Little bald-faced sorrel?"

I said, "That's the one."

When I asked what his problem was, she said, "When he was very young he fell down at the first barrel; people ran over and covered him up and everyone was yelling and screaming . . . and he doesn't want to talk about it." Once I learned it was just fear that was messing Giz up, I decided to give him the benefit of the doubt and work with him to see if we could get through it. There was just so much talent there it became a challenge to see if I could get it out of him.

It was frustrating for a long time because he'd win a first-place cheque one day, run down the wall the next and win another first-place cheque the day after that. But we did eventually get things straightened around. We've been to the Canadian Finals together eight times and won Denver, San Angelo and Rapid City in the States. When I say we've solved the problem, that isn't quite accurate. If I don't ride him right, he'll go down the wall with me, even today.

It's circumstances that make him do it, so I always have to be aware of what's going on around me. He hates alleys leading into arenas so I have to kind of nurse him through those. Sometimes he gets nervous and doesn't breathe. And if I run too hard at the first barrel, that blows his mind too. He's just a horse who's scared of everything. That's something he never got over. The good thing about him is that where most horses that run down the wall do it rodeo after rodeo, Giz is different. If he was to do that today, I wouldn't even worry because he might not do it again for a year.

Riding him is an adventure, though. Last year at Morris he took a big flying leap just as we crossed the line to start the race, and he was heading for the left-hand barrel. We normally go to the right-hand barrel first but that option was gone so I thought, "Okay, let's see what happens." I wound up splitting second and third there and got a huge cheque on a horse that hadn't run to the left in at least four years.

Two years ago at Lea Park where there is a really long alley, I finally got him close to the arena and he took that same flying leap, then ran as fast as he could go right down the centre of the arena, then turned and ran just as hard straight back out again. We never even glanced at a barrel. The cowboys on the fence were almost falling off they were laughing so hard. I'm sure the people watching that rodeo were wondering what on earth Giz and I were all about. Actually, I was wondering the same thing.

You can't help but like the guy because he's such a nice horse to be around. He loads good, he travels well, he eats, he doesn't kick, he talks to you; he's just a happy horse except when he's in the alley before a barrel race. This past year he's developed some foot problem and I'm really worried about him. The injuries may be serious enough that I won't be able to compete on him again. That will be hard.

My new horse, Ace, was $30,000 American. That's the most I've ever paid for a horse. It seems there are a lot more girls willing to pay big money for horses these days as opposed to taking young horses and making them into barrel horses. In a lot of ways it makes sense to try to buy a horse that's ready, or almost ready to compete. The problem is you might go through ten horses before you come up with that one good one. And each of those ten probably took $3,500 to $6,500 to find out that it wasn't good enough. For that reason, it makes sense to go out and pay the money for a horse that's proven.

Not that putting out the big money is a guarantee. First of all there aren't that many really good horses out there, especially in Canada where there are only a few people, like Isabelle Miller and Rayel Robinson, who are training and putting out those good ones. As a result more people are going to the States to find horses. But that's iffy, too. When you do go to Texas or somewhere shopping for a horse, you might get on twenty but you can only try them in their home arenas. You really have no idea what that horse is going to be like when you get it back to Canada. It's different if it's a horse of Rayel's that you've seen all year and know is a good one.

Even then not every girl can jump on a particular horse — even a good one — and click right off the bat. Some horses just work really well for one person and not at all for another. A horse might get passed around two or three times before it gets to someone who really knows how to ride it to win.

There are no sure things in barrel racing. I guess it's a darn good thing we like these horses as much as we do. It could get awfully frustrating if we didn't.

* KELLY *

All the time I was growing up and the other kids were buying baseball cards or Nintendo games, I was saving my money to buy a cow. Once I got one bought, I'd start saving to buy another one. I wasn't very old — eleven, I think — when I got my first bull. He was a yearling that came from [the late pickup man] Gerald Shockey. Gerald had sold some calves and this big brindle was in with them. He ended up at Wes Yanke's place and Wes called me.

I talked my mom into driving me over there to get him. That bull was so mean we couldn't get him loaded. I had to buy a Holstein steer to put with him just so we could get him into the trailer. I'd planned to use him to practise on because he was small, but all he wanted to do was mangle me. I ended up practising on the Holstein for two years.

That damn bull did get me my first stock contracting cheque though. My neighbour, Jay Lundy, arranged to take him to Regina's Agribition Rodeo to use in the bullfight. [World champion bullfighter] Greg Rohmer fought him and was 83 points. But that bull never did buck, not once.

Wilf Gerlitz was one guy who was really good to me. He sent me great bulls like Double Ott and Blaster to breed my six or seven cows to. It's the heifer calves I kept from those breedings that are the foundation of the herd I have today.

My bulls are like my kids to me. I take them to a rodeo, and from then on I'm probably no different from that mom or dad watching their kid play hockey. I want those bulls to do well — not for me, but for themselves. There's another similarity too. I don't dare brag on my bulls. As soon as I do that, they're sure to go out there and suck just like when a dad brags up his kid, sure enough that kid is going to have the worst game ever. I think it's a Murphy's Law thing.

I've often thought about what it would be like to draw one of my own bulls at a rodeo. I think I'd be cheering for both of us.

And heck, we'd both look good if I won. But that son-of-a-gun better not even think about biting the hand that feeds!

When I think about bulls, I think about the great bulls. In the same way that there's rodeo in my history, there's also rodeo in theirs. They've been bred and grown up to be bucking bulls. I have a lot of respect for them, respect that comes in two ways. First, I respect bulls as athletes in the same way I respect a great bull rider. These bulls are in shape, they're fed right; they are fit to perform just as any athlete is.

Second, I respect their power, their strength. That's when I'm reminded that we cowboys are the inferior ones in the contest. If it came down to a test of strength alone, the cowboy would come in second every time. When I ride, I believe it comes down to trying to match the bull's moves. There's no way I can overpower or outmuscle him so I have to outwit and outmanoeuvre him. That outwitting part isn't all that easy.

I've heard people refer to "those dumb bulls." I can't honestly say I've met a dumb one yet. I think anybody who spends a couple of days around these animals will quickly realize that each one has his own unique personality. And they are smart, especially the older bulls. It amazes me how smart they are. A lot of them actually figure out what works best to throw a cowboy off. They'll know where the out-gate is at a rodeo they've never been to before. They figure that out too by watching the other bulls and where they go. Dumb? I don't think so.

As a bull rider and a person who raises bulls for rodeo, I'm concerned about what people think of our sport. I believe there are a lot of people who are really sincere in how they feel about animal rights, for example. And I think we should take their concerns seriously. So far I think rodeo's idea of a response to people who express a concern about the animals in rodeo is to call them names. I think we can do better than that.

I like the approach [American stock contractors] Harper and Morgan are using. They have signs up at their rodeos inviting people to view the livestock before and after the rodeo. The Professional Rodeo Cowboys Association made a good move when it outlawed hotshots (electric prods). People hate those things, and the PRCA listened to what they were saying. That's good.

I have to say — and I really mean this — I would love to live the life of my bulls. My young bulls are out with their mothers their first summer. Then when they're weaned they go to Jim and Myra Greig's place. Jim loves having young bulls around his place. He's got my Edward Scissorhands calves practically made into pets.

I don't buck my bulls until they're two-year-olds. Then they'll buck maybe twenty times over the next two years. In other words, in the first four years of their lives, my bulls work about 160 seconds. Proven bulls — if they're busy — don't buck much more than that . . . maybe twenty or thirty times a year.

More and more contractors are realizing what it takes to keep these bulls bucking. That's good feed and plenty of it. It's just not good business to skimp on that end of the operation. We have a lot invested in these animals and we need them to perform well if we want a return on our investment. There's nothing that makes me happier than knowing my animals are eating good. You get out of them what you put into them. I want my bulls to be hard, with not a bunch of gut, and I want them built for speed. They're no different than us. If I spend my time lying on the couch and eating potato chips, I'm not going to be much good at what I do.

It's not uncommon for a contractor to pay $5,000 or $7,500 American for a really good bull. So if that guy buys five bulls and spends $25,000 or $30,000, it wouldn't make any sense at all to treat those animals badly.

Animal rights people like to get on the travel part of a rodeo animal's life. Here again, when we haul animals it only makes sense to have them travel in something they're comfortable in and that they won't hurt themselves in. I know that most stock contractors load their animals and hustle to the rodeo so they can get them off the trucks and into the pens.

It's fun to watch old bulls load. They walk up there and stand in about the same place every time. They know what the deal is. It's like when we used to go on field trips as kids. When we got back on the bus somebody would yell, "Same seats!" The toughest kids always got to sit in the back. It's no different with bulls. The toughest bull picks the spot he wants and the others work around him.

The other area of concern for non-rodeo people is the flank, which is the strap or rope we put on bulls to help them buck. I've heard all the stories about how we put barbed wire on their testicles. That's so ridiculous I wonder how someone with any intelligence at all can say something like that. What animal is going to leap and buck and spin if it is in pain?

The people who are saying those things shouldn't take my word for it. They need to make a point of going behind the chutes and seeing for themselves what really goes on. Or they can go out in the pastures and see young colts and calves jumping and bucking just for fun. It's what they do to play.

A while back Austin and I were at a guy's place in Oklahoma. We drove out in a field where he had about fifteen head of bucking bred cows. We sat there watching their calves for a long time and you wouldn't believe the fun they were having, running around that field and jumping two or three feet in the air. It's that natural to them. Bucking is in their breeding, in the same way running is bred into the Thoroughbreds down on those Kentucky horse farms. That breeding is becoming so fine-tuned now that a breeder can produce a pen of calves and have only one or two that don't buck and spin.

What we ask bulls to do in the rodeo arena is not unnatural to them. In fact, I'm convinced it's the most natural thing in the world. They want to get that guy off. If that wasn't the case, why would they quit bucking after he's off, which is something a lot of them do.

On the other hand, there are some bulls that keep bucking even after they've thrown the bull rider off. A good example of that is Jiminy Cricket. That is the tryingest bull I've ever seen. That little sucker plays rodeo all day every day. He bucks around there after the ride and all the way out of the arena. It sure isn't because he's flanked tight; it's because he loves what he's doing. He's playing.

When I watch bulls after they have bucked cowboys off, I get a definite sense that they're enjoying themselves. You can see it in the way they behave. There's a pride in them and you can see it as they're moving around — heads up, looking around and saying to the world, "Hey, look at me, I did pretty good, eh?"

Actually, some of them enjoy themselves a little *too* much for my liking.

✳ DUANE ✳

If I ever get reincarnated I'd like to come back as a great bronc. Bucking horses are like all the animals in rodeo — they get fed the best, they don't work all that much and most of the time their lives are like it was for horses on the open range years ago. They're at their home ranch out in the pasture with the herd and it's right back to the way they lived when horses were wild and roamed free. There's a social order, with the older horses as the bosses and new arrivals to the herd at the bottom of the totem pole. And they have their buddies out there, the horses they like to be around. It's comical to watch them.

I really believe they enjoy going to the rodeos and the ones that get left behind, some of them are pretty mad about it. I have another theory too. I can't prove it but I think when they're back in the pens or at the home place after the rodeo, they somehow communicate to each other how their day went, who rode them that day and what happened. At least that's how it looks to me. Who knows, maybe they're as good at telling stories as cowboys are.

It only makes sense to look after the animals of rodeo. These horses, for example, are our livelihood and it wouldn't make sense for us to want to hurt them. I'm often asked about the flank strap. I really think the flank strap is important to the protection of horse and rider. A horse has a far greater chance of injuring itself when it's just running out of control than when it's bucking. Kicking at the flank slows them down. And there's not a lot of pressure on the flank. If people look at the pictures in the bronc riding, they'll see daylight between the flank and the horse's belly. It's an irritant and they want to get rid of it, just like they want that cowboy off their backs, but I can say very truthfully that there is absolutely no pain involved in having a flank strap on a horse.

When I was living in a trailer on the rodeo grounds here in Innisfail, the horses would come in a few days early. I loved going out there with some oats and spending time with them. It seemed to me that they all had their own personalities. There was one old campaigner out there, his name was Wall Street. I'd had him a few years before in the Novice Bronc Riding but now he was a lot older. I jumped up on his back out there in the pasture and boy, did that make him mad. It was like I'd insulted him.

Some horses are outlaws, no doubt about it. They're not a lot of fun to draw. I remember a bronc that belonged to the Cervi outfit down in the States. His name was Mr. Tibbs and he was noted for biting people. He was smart about it, though. He didn't bother unless he could really get hold of somebody. It always came when guys were least expecting it and thought they were going to get by him this time. There's teeth marks on bronc riders all over North America that came from Mr. Tibbs.

I had him in San Antone, and George Strait was up on the back of the chute. He got a little close and was looking over the back of the chute. I kept waiting for that old bronc to reach up and grab George's hat. But the horse was more interested in flesh and George got out of there without having to leave some behind.

Another horse with an interesting attitude was a character named Casino. He'd stand in the chute like he was sleeping, but when they cracked that gate he exploded. It was like he was saying, "Okay, go ahead and get your stuff on because in a few minutes I'm gonna make your life unpleasant." The thing is there are horses that try to outsmart the bronc rider. They'll try to mess that guy up in the chute by leaning on one side or the other or they'll run a little ways before they break. They have lots of little gimmicks and they use them all.

I had a neat experience with a tremendous horse up here in Canada. His name was Come Apart and I'd had him in the Novice event somewhere. Some of these broncs are broke saddle horses before they get to the rodeo arena and he was one of them. We had him up here for our bucking horse sale in '77 and I decided I'd ride him around the ring at one of our regular horse sales the day before the bucking horse sale. I rode with just a piece of binder twine and he was great. I did the same thing at the bucking horse sale. Wayne Vold bought him, and Come Apart went on to become one of the outstanding broncs for years.

The thing about riding broncs is that it's not always the best score that was your best ride. The money is almost always won on the nice horses. What made me feel good was when I got on a rank bronc — one of those ones that's really hard to ride — and was still able to do the things I wanted to do on the horse. When I could make it work and still live on the edge with that kind of horse, it was pretty darn satisfying.

One in particular stands out in my mind as that kind of ride. I had a horse named Roan Angel in San Angelo, Texas, in the early nineties. She was a big, strong mare and all the bronc riders had a lot of respect for her. It was like she was saying, "Here I am, come at me" every time somebody got on her.

That day she got me up on top of my saddle, which is an expression we use to describe the fact that the rider is way out there and maybe a little out of control. It's easy to quit and safety-up on a ride like that, but I didn't. I rode her every jump as aggressively and as well as I could. When I got off her — I think I placed and won a little on her that day — I was mighty proud. I don't know if anybody else in the building even noticed, but I knew I'd just made one of the best rides of my life.

I always found the toughest horses to ride were the ones that kept their heads high in the air so that you really had to lift on your rein to ride them. The really rank ones were almost always unpredictable too. Usually they were a little older and a little smarter. Wayne Vold used to have a horse in his string called Sarcee Sorrel. He was a horse that a lot of guys just tried to float by and not get their spurs into him to make him mad.

But when guys turned their toes out and really went at him, he'd let them stay on for a few jumps and then it was just as if he said, "Okay, buddy, that's enough." Then he'd set the rider up and fire him out of there. When he was having his day, there weren't a lot of guys that were going to get by him.

Kingsway, the Franklin bronc — the one that was on the stamp — was pretty special too but for a different reason. I think of him as just an outstanding athlete. He bucked an awful lot of guys off but there were days when you could ride him. It wasn't that he was having a bad day, it's just that he wasn't as rank and impossible on those days as the others. Another horse that gave me trouble was one called Sagebrush. He was a horse of the Keslers' and as hard to ride as any. I made the whistle on him a few times but I never once made the pickup man.

If the contest was just to stay on their backs, we could ride them all. But in the Bronc Riding, if you don't spur you don't win and that's the big equalizer. The more we expose ourselves and turn those toes out east and west, there's not a lot holding onto that saddle. The other factor is the different styles of different riders. Some guys could get along with certain horses better than other guys mostly because of the way they rode.

The horses that we really want to get on for the money are the ones that give us a good, honest shot coming out of the chute and have that snap to them so you can actually feel them kicking out behind you during the ride. If you can get in time with that kind, the riding gets pretty easy. Timing is so important, and a lot of those nice horses will let the rider get in time with them. And when they hit the ground, it's not with the same degree of power as those really tough ones.

I guess if I had to pick one to get on when the money was on the line, that horse would be Papa Smurf of the Calgary Stampede string. He is so great day in and day out that you know that if you don't stub your toe or mess up with him, things should turn out just fine.

But my all-time favourite horse would have to be a little mare of Calgary's called Rolly Polly. I think I had a string of six wins in a row on her back in the mid-eighties. We just seemed to fit each other, and every time I found out I'd drawn her I was licking my chops.

I think every guy has his favourites and I know there are some guys who have a great old bronc or two out on their place as kind of a rest home project. The reason is simple — these horses mean a lot to the cowboys who try to ride them. We respect them and we genuinely like most of them. So I guess it isn't surprising that some guys like to be able to look out the window and see a horse out in the pasture that they rode ten years ago at Calgary or Red Deer or Hanna. It's a nice memory for the cowboy and a good home for an old horse in its retirement years.

Miles and Miles of Miles and Miles

One of the facts of rodeo life is that in order to compete, one must get to the rodeo and back again. The mind-numbing miles, middle-of-the-night stops to let horses off trailers, cheap motels and bad fast-food joints add up to the least appealing feature of the rodeo competitor's life. It is not unusual for cowboys and cowgirls to travel twenty-five or thirty hours to get to a rodeo, then spend only a couple of hours there — just long enough to compete, load the horses and grab a burger before setting off again. It's dangerous — much of the driving is done at night and it's my guess that more lives are lost getting to and from rodeos than in the arenas themselves. And most of all — after the first several hundred thousand kilometres — it's just plain boring. Yet few of today's rodeo contestants resent it; most actually look forward to the next trip to the next rodeo in the next town with something akin to anticipation. Oh, they do all they can to make the miles tolerable, even enjoyable and are very Y2K about travelling. The cell phone and organizer are close at hand, food and drink (often bottled water, not pop, and surprisingly little junk food) is within reaching distance and a well-stocked CD case is always at the ready (with Amanda Marshall, Steve Earle, some early Lynyrd Skynyrd and maybe even the soundtrack from Grease taking their place alongside Shania and Clint). Yet, in one respect, the cowboys and cowgirls of the new millennium are no different from their counterparts of fifty years ago. They accept the travel as part of the game; yes, the miles exact a toll, but it's a toll that every competitor willingly pays.

✳ M O N I C A ✳

It probably sounds strange to people who aren't used to putting on the miles in their own lives that we do, but a lot of us enjoy it. It's kind of a high to be getting in the truck and heading off down the road again, not so much because of the driving itself but for what we're driving to. I guess it's different when I'm not winning; the miles seem to be a lot longer then. But if I'm doing well or even reasonably well, I look forward to loading my horse and hitting the highway. I've been on so many roads so many times that I can actually anticipate the next corner on some obscure highway in the middle of nowhere that only the locals and rodeo people know about.

We do a lot of our travelling with the same people every weekend and it gets to be a lot of fun. If one of the people in the rig isn't doing well, there are three people trying to analyze what's wrong instead of just one. Over the years I've travelled thousands of miles with Leslie Schlosser and Charlotte Schmidt. Both of them have been to the NFR and have had a lot of success over the years. I remember in 1996, during the month of May, we won over $40,000 between the three of us. That's not a bad haul coming out of one rig. At Innisfail that year we finished one-two-three and for a while we were first, second and fourth in terms of money won in Canada.

If the travelling combination is working, it's a good idea to stay with it. When we're on the road, we're not just travelling together, we're living together. There's a closeness there, a bond that people feel for each other when they go so many miles together. It has to be that way and if it isn't, the combination will change pretty quickly. With three people scrunched into the living quarters of a horse trailer, it doesn't take long to find out if somebody can't stand somebody else.

We look after each other the same way we would if we were travelling with sisters. When Charlotte and I found out Leslie had a problem with diabetes, we changed our travel program to help her out. We made sure Les drove the first shift before she got tired. And we adjusted our eating and drinking habits on the road as well. Charlotte used to have a couple of bags of candy on the front seat while she was driving. She ditched the candy and we cut out pop and coffee because we knew Leslie couldn't have those things. It wasn't like we felt we were making a big sacrifice. It was just something we wanted to do for a friend and travelling partner.

We learn the other person's quirks as well. When Charlotte had a bad run, she needed a twenty-minute cooling-off period. So we steered clear of her for that twenty minutes and then she was fine.

Being on the road as much as we are and seeing as many idiot drivers as we do, road rage does take over once in a while. But there are places where giving someone a piece of your mind is a really bad idea. A couple of years ago we were on our way to Houston from Tucson and a guy cut us off. I was all for rolling down my window and telling the jerk what I thought of his driving and maybe a few other things too. Judy Myllymaki, an American cowgirl, was driving and she made it real clear that in that part of the world, when somebody cuts you off, you keep your mouth shut.

There have been times I didn't think I'd make the trip in the time I had. A few years ago I was travelling with Charlotte and Judy's daughter, Rachel Myllymaki. We were in Rapid City on Thursday night and we made the Finals, which meant we had to come back there on the weekend. In the meantime we had to go to Minneapolis on Friday. Debbie Renger (she was Debbie Guelly then) was following us and she was by herself in her outfit. It was a really foggy night and the road was sheer ice. There was another rig in front of us, and I made sure I kept the lights of that horse trailer in sight. Those lights were about all I could see.

At one point we came to a hill, and as we climbed this hill the outfit in front of us went slower and slower. Eventually I was afraid that we were going to stall so I pulled out and passed. Passing in those conditions was crazy but I figure stalling in the middle of the road was crazier. Debbie didn't realize we had passed the trailer that had been in front of us. She kept following the red lights in front of her, which she thought belonged to us but were actually on the trailer we had passed.

Debbie followed that horse trailer right into a yard, still not knowing it was someone else. It turned out to be some rodeo people, Troy and Marti Pruitt from down there, and out of that meeting Debbie and the Pruitts became great friends. In the meantime, we sat at the side of the road a little farther on waiting for Debbie. Of course she never did show up, and we finally went on. We were awful glad to see her the next day when she arrived at Minneapolis with Troy and Marti. We ran that night in Minneapolis, then the next night were back in Rapid City for the Finals there. After the rodeo in Rapid City, we drove all that night and the next day to get to San Antonio where we were up in slack Monday and Tuesday morning. Then we drove to El Paso for the slack Wednesday and Thursday morning.

And that was it for me, I'd had enough. I borrowed Debbie's rig and she jumped in with Charlotte and Rachel. I left El Paso at one o'clock Thursday afternoon and got home at seven o'clock Saturday morning. I kept stopping to phone Bob at home and he'd say, "Where are you?"

My answers were always something like "I don't know. Colorado, I think."

Speeding tickets are a fact of life for people who travel as much as we do, often with tricky time lines to get places. Leslie, Charlotte and I were coming back from Kamloops in my truck. Leslie was driving and just the other side of Golden, B.C., a cop pulled up beside us and started yelling at us through his foghorn, "Pull over! Pull over!"

Leslie pulled over, and the cop came to the window to ask her for her driver's licence. She hopped out of the truck to look behind the seat but couldn't find her purse. She told the cop she must have left it in the hotel room in Kamloops. The cop wrote her out a ticket for $175 but then wrote "Warning" across it. I guess he was being a nice guy.

"Now slow down," he said. "You went through here yesterday and you were speeding then." I tried to tell him it wasn't us but he said, "Sure it was you, all the same junk is still in the sleeper."

We left and headed off toward Golden, which was only about thirteen kilometres away. We got right to the edge of Golden and the RCMP had another radar trap set up. The same cop nailed us again. He came up to the window, took one look at Leslie and turned to the other cop who was with him. "She's all yours," was all he said.

One of the sneakier cop things that ever happened to us was in Washington. A cop pulled four vehicles over; we were the last of the four. Charlotte was driving and the cop came to our vehicle first. He said, "I'm sorry, but I need to know how fast that guy in front of you was going. I can't get more than two on the radar and that's the guy I want."

Ever helpful, Charlotte said, "Well, I was going seventy-five."

He wrote her out a ticket right on the spot. Charlotte fumed about that for weeks.

I was travelling with Shellee and Darren Shaw one time, and as we were coming into Calgary, the cops had a check stop set up and were waving people onto an off-ramp. Shellee was going so fast she knew she wouldn't make the off-ramp so she just kept going. She looked back and cops were scrambling to get in their cars to chase after her. She finally got stopped, and one of the cops came up to the truck, a little unhappy. He told her she was doing something over 140 clicks. Shellee tried to tell him the truck we were in wouldn't go that fast but he wasn't buying that. The cop launched into a lengthy lecture about her driving. Finally Darren, who was sitting in the passenger seat, leaned forward and said, "Excuse me, could you just write her the ticket so we can get going."

That led to a pretty heated discussion between Darren and the cop. All this time I was in the trailer (which is illegal too), hoping this cop wouldn't check back there, which would have cost us more money.

Music is important for anybody who spends a lot of time on the road. We all have our favourite stuff. When I'm really tired or sick of driving, I crank up one of my Billy Joe Royal cassettes. His music always picks me up. He's had some hits; one of them was "Down in the Boondocks." I think he's the greatest. The only trouble is it doesn't seem like very many people in rodeo even know who he is.

Recently one of my barrel-racing friends, Merry Ann Stoney, came up to me all excited. "Monica, I came across a whole bunch of tapes by that guy you like and I bought all of them for you." I was just as excited as she was because I'd looked all over the place for Billy Joe Royal tapes and could never find any.

She brought out the tapes, and that's when my excitement ended. The cassettes Merry Ann had been so proud of tracking down were by Billy Joel. I think she got me pretty well his complete works. "Merry Ann," I said, "what are these? The guy I like is *Billy Joe Royal*."

We had a good laugh about it, and I'm still listening to those same almost worn-out Billy Joe Royal tapes.

Sometimes things happen that a person can't believe even as they're happening. Judy Myllymaki and I were in Salt Lake one year. It was the middle of the afternoon and the rodeo was at seven that night. It was really hot so we thought we'd go into the arena where it was cooler. We got in there; there wasn't a soul in the place so we picked out a couple of seats and sat down to read our books.

After a while we noticed two old men wandering our way. They were wearing Panama hats, short pants and flowered shirts and were carrying little woven baskets with handles. They strolled around the place for a while, then came over to where Judy and I were sitting. They looked at us for a while, then one of the men said, "Excuse me, you're in our seats."

I couldn't believe it. All the seats in that place; it was five hours before the rodeo and the only other people in the place are telling us we're in their seats. And we were. I had to look at their tickets before I'd believe it. Someday I'm going to draw a cartoon of that moment.

✳ KELLY ✳

The first year I rode bulls I was too young to drive so I'd take the Greyhound bus to the first rodeo and then catch rides with other competitors after that. The only part of that deal that didn't always work out was getting home after the last rodeo. There were times I didn't make it back on Sunday night. That was more of a problem for my parents and teachers than it was for me. I always felt that a rodeo weekend ran from Thursday to Tuesday. That left Wednesday for being at home, gathering up clean clothes — not too many, I wasn't much of a fashion statement in those days — then getting back to the bus depot in time to start the next expedition.

Like most people in this business I've been in a few slumps. In the spring of 1995 over a thirty-one-day period, I'd been on more than twenty bulls and stayed on exactly one. I was so cold I couldn't decide whether to retire or slash my wrists. I was leaning toward the wrist-slashing but I figured as bad as things were going I'd probably fail at that too. The only thing I was sure of was that things couldn't get worse. I was wrong.

I had a Bull Riding to get to in Beaumont, Texas. I headed out from Vernon, Texas, early in the morning. There had been freezing rain the night before but I was confident that, being from Canada, I could handle the road conditions. I made it exactly two blocks before I ran into a Grand Cherokee driven by a lawyer. Real good choice of guys to run into. Once the vehicles were sorted out, I walked back to the house, borrowed a car and set off again. This time I made it to Beaumont but wished I hadn't. I bucked off so fast most of the fans never knew I was there. I spent so little time on that bull, he must have thought he was a turnout.

I did manage to stay even-tempered about the way my month was going. I was mad *all* the time. I drove all that night to get back to Vernon. I was about five miles from home when the next disaster struck. Five o'clock in the morning — highway patrol. I remember thinking, "What the hell is he doing out of bed at this hour?"

He got me doing 100 mph in a 55 mph zone. Three hundred dollars later I was on my way. I got home and went to bed for the day, partly to sleep and partly to hide. I had a Bull Riding in Ardmore, Oklahoma, that night. I got up about four o'clock in the afternoon to shower and get ready to go. As I was getting dressed, I realized the only pair of clean socks I had was a pair of black ones I'd bought for Justin Keeley's wedding. That was the only time I'd had them on and I hadn't really planned on wearing them ever again.

I thought about going with a pair of dirty white socks but then I thought to myself, "Hell, if I'm going to ride like a poindexter, I might as well look like one." I got to Ardmore, won the Bull Riding, picked up a cheque for $5,000 and retired the black socks.

My college roommate was Roudy Bauer, an Australian. They put us together at college because no one could understand either one of us. It was our freshman year and we decided to enter a rodeo in Montgomery, Alabama. It was a good rodeo. Harper and Morgan were the contractors; there was $5,000 added money, which we figured a couple of first-year college students could use. But I should have known an Australian and a Canadian might have some trouble finding our way around the southern United States.

I had developed a theory that I could drive across any state in America in three hours. So I worked out our travel schedule according to my three-hour formula and away we went. We left at eight in the morning for what I had calculated as a nine-hour drive (three states). "We'll be there with lots of time to spare," I told Roudy.

The journey went okay for a while but eventually it seemed like we were going to run out of time long before we ran out of road. Roudy was starting to question my geography skills so I agreed that maybe we should pull over and buy a map. That was when I discovered I had totally forgotten to factor in Mississippi.

That left us no choice but to pick up the pace considerably now that Mississippi had completely screwed up my travel itinerary. There we were rolling down that Interstate in rain that was coming down sideways. We were going so fast we were skipping like a rock down that road.

Talk about a photo-finish — they were bucking bulls when we got there. But we made it and got on. Unfortunately neither of us dipped into the $5,000 prize money. Roudy was pretty upset but I figured the trip was worth it, what with everything we'd learned about geography in the American south and all.

Cowboys call the July long weekend "Cowboy Christmas" because of all the rodeos and opportunities to make money. First there are the Canadian rodeos over the July 1 part of the holiday, and then we cruise right into the American fourth of July and a whole bunch more. But the travel can be a little tough, to say the least.

For my first Cowboy Christmas experience, I realized I was going to need some help driving. So I recruited Austin. He was willing enough even though he'd never been farther from home than Great Falls and hadn't heard of any of the places we'd be going to.

I finished up the Canadian run at Ponoka, met Austin there and away we went. Our first stop was St. Paul, Oregon, just south of Portland. I got flung off my bull there, whacked in the head in the process and thrown into a bush. There aren't a lot of rodeo arenas with bushes in them but St. Paul had bushes. The bull was pretty small and he was in those bushes with me, wanting to hook me but luckily he couldn't find me.

We loaded up after that experience and headed for Eugene, Oregon, where I was entered the same day. The trick with Eugene is just to find the rodeo grounds. We couldn't. By the time we did I was sure we'd missed the Bull Riding and we would have except there was some kind of concert part way through the rodeo that delayed the Bull Riding just long enough for us to get there.

I rode that bull and placed on him but he threw me right at the whistle. I hit the chutes in midair, and it was just like the cartoons where the guy slides down after hitting the brick wall. I ended up in a sitting position leaning against the chutes thinking, "I'm glad this day is over."

The next day my ace driver and I hit the trail again — for Santa Fe, New Mexico. We drove all day without taking a break and once again got there just in time. I was so sore from the beating I'd taken in Oregon and sitting in that car all that time that Austin and I had agreed if nobody there knew us, he was going to ride as Kelly Armstrong. Just before the Bull Riding Mark Cain and Lynn Upmore showed up. They're bull riders and knew both of us so the substitute rider plan was out the window.

I hadn't had time to ask anybody about my bull. All I knew was that his number was one, he was red and he was small, which back in those days I thought was a good thing. I noticed that they had saved me for the last, which I also took as a positive sign. As I was getting on, I was thinking, "Wow, this sucker must be good." But about four or five seconds into the ride, I realized I was on the fighting bull. Right then about all I wanted was to be back in Canada. He got me down, ran over me and definitely did my body no good whatsoever.

The next day I was up at Wolf Point, Montana. Getting there was an even longer trek than the Oregon to Santa Fe run had been. Austin had started making comments about the planning part of my rodeo program but I figured what did he know. When we arrived at Wolf Point, the first thing I found out was that I had a bull with the number one again. I was starting to wonder if being a professional bull rider was a wise career choice.

I was almost afraid to ask about the bull because of the bad time I'd had with the last number one. I hadn't slept most of the night before from thinking about the fighting bull in Santa Fe. Luckily the bull in Wolf Point didn't fight. He also didn't buck and I marked a 67.

We had picked up Roudy Bauer in Santa Fe and taken him with us to Wolf Point. We got Roudy to buy us some beer. I was so sore I figured I needed a few beers to console myself. We wound up having quite a few beers, and when we got to the border, Roudy, the Australian, was driving the car with Alberta licence plates while Austin and I had the back seat down and were sleeping with our feet in the trunk.

The border guy took one look at us and told Roudy to park the car and bring everyone inside. I figured the situation might be touchy so I went in to do a little PR with the border guys. Austin followed me in, grumpy from being woken up. Well, actually he was stomping mad — no boots but stomping just the same. He got in there and right away demanded to know what the holdup was. That was the wrong approach, especially considering the way we looked and smelled. Pretty soon they had us in different rooms and were giving us the *NYPD Blue* treatment. Eventually they let us go and we raced off for a rodeo in Benalto, Alberta, not much more than a rock's throw away compared to some of the distances we'd been covering.

I hadn't slept in a bed in a week and it had been almost as long since we'd seen a shower. I'd been beat up, stomped on, hadn't made a whole lot of money and I had a hangover. It seemed to me that Cowboy Christmas wasn't at all like the real thing.

✳ DUANE ✳

Like a lot of rodeo kids, I got initiated into the travel part of rodeo pretty early on. Most of the time during my steer riding days I was a passenger . . . but not always. I remember one night I jumped into a car with my uncle Franklin, Gerald Reber, Gary Logan, and Jim Gladstone heading for a rodeo in Saskatoon, Saskatchewan. I was maybe thirteen or fourteen. Those guys had a big poker game going before we left and wanted to keep it going while we made our way to the rodeo. That meant I'd have to do the driving.

We were in Gerald's car — a station wagon with a two-horse trailer behind us — and Gerald was a big man so the driver's seat was dished out pretty good. I had to look through the steering wheel because I couldn't see over the top of it. I drove all the way to Saskatoon. We went awful slow but those guys didn't care. They were in the back with a spare gas tank between them, smoking cigars and having a great time. The IOUs were up into the thousands by the end of the night.

Rumours are a big deal in rodeo. I was involved in a classic. Guy Shapka and I had taken my airplane up to a rodeo in northern Alberta. After the rodeo, we flew out of there with another planeload of cowboys behind us a ways. The weather wasn't real good. We talked on the radio back and forth with the guys in the other plane until they decided to land in Whitecourt for the night. I told them I was going to try to make it home. Guy and I continued on for a while but the weather got worse. We decided to land in Drayton Valley, leave the airplane there and borrow a car from Clayton Hines, a friend and retired bronc rider.

Clayton lent us a vehicle and we finally got to my house very late that night. Guy was sleeping downstairs and I was upstairs. I had to get up at 5:00 a.m. to catch a commercial flight to Caldwell, Idaho, where I'd made the Finals. I'd set an alarm for Guy. He had a little more time to play with because he only had to get to Pincher Creek the next day where he had the best horse in the draw. Guy slept through the alarm and didn't make it to Pincher Creek. But the guys in that other plane from the night before did get there.

When they saw that Guy hadn't showed up to get on a great horse, they told people he'd been in a plane with me that was flying into bad weather. The story went around the coffee stand a couple of times and it wasn't long before word was out that a plane was down and Guy and I were in it. We got a few strange (and relieved) looks when we both reappeared a day or so later.

I guess some of my travelling was different from the way a lot of competitors got to rodeos in that I flew quite a bit of the time. Something I realized early on was that the best instrument in my plane was my gut. When the weather's coming down and those power lines aren't very far below, it doesn't matter that all the guys in the plane are wanting to keep going. I learned early on that when my gut feeling was "It's time to get the hell out of here," then it was time to get the hell out of there.

I think it's the same way in rodeo and in life too. I often listened to my gut — I guess some might call it common sense — in my rodeo career and in the rest of my life. I think it was when I didn't listen sometimes that I made mistakes.

A time that was pretty special to me was during the Iran crisis of the early eighties when Ken Taylor, the Canadian ambassador, smuggled some Americans to safety. I was down in the United States at the winter rodeos and everywhere I drove I saw little signs in coffee shop windows and all over the place thanking Canada and Canadians. I went to a rodeo in Baton Rouge right around that time. They brought out the Canadian flag at the start of the rodeo, and the people there gave us a standing ovation. All the Canadians who competed that night got a huge cheer no matter how we did.

When people spend as much time together as we do, there are bound to be pranks . . . a lot of pranks. One of my favourites was when we were in Tulsa, Oklahoma, in the spring of the year, which happens to be tornado season down there. There were five or six of us holed up in a motor hotel. The veterans in the crowd were both bronc riders, Rick Smith and me. The other guys were rookies, and rodeo's no different than most sports as far as how rookies are treated. Rick and I had gone down to the lounge to get something to eat and the other guys stayed up in the room.

While we were eating, we noticed it was getting pretty grey and dark outside. About that time a bulletin came on the TV saying there was a tornado watch in the area. We got the desk clerk to call up to the room to say the tornado was just down the street and the guys should take cover. He told them to pull the mattresses off the bed and climb into the bathtub. When we got up to the room, there were the rookies with the mattresses stripped off the bed. They weren't *in* the bathtub but they were right beside it ready to take the dive.

Another prank victim was Rod (Moose) Warren. It was in the early nineties and a bunch of us put the judges up to making a big production of measuring his saddle like it was illegal. Moose got hostile in a hurry. The judges told him they were acting on instructions from the CPRA office. Moose had had a run-in with the office not that long before, and it's a good thing none of the CPRA administrators were around right at that moment. When Moose realized he'd been had, it took him a while but he finally laughed about it and admitted we'd got him pretty good.

I got Denny Hay too. We were travelling across to Bremerton, Washington, on the ferry. Denny is a small-town prairie boy and hadn't seen a lot of the world back then. I knew he loved to hunt and fish so I had him primed before we got on the ferry that they rented fishing tackle for people to use on the crossing. I told him people often fished off the back of the boat. As fast as those things go, I don't know what Denny thought he might catch, but he spent a fair amount of time trying to track down one of those rental fishing poles.

I used to come up through Vancouver when I rodeoed over on the west coast because it was easier to catch a flight into Calgary from there than from Salt Lake. I'd get into Vancouver about five o'clock in the morning and hang out at the airport until it was time for my flight to Calgary. Whenever I flew commercial I kept my saddle with me. On one of those trips I had a little time so I found a nice soft rug down by one of the baggage claims and stretched out with my head on my saddle to get some sleep.

The next thing I knew I was awake and there were flashing lights all over the place and the biggest racket I'd ever heard. It turned out a 747 from Tokyo had arrived a few minutes before. Here were a couple of hundred Japanese tourists and in their first few minutes in Canada what do they see but a cowboy with his saddle stretched out there on the floor. Suddenly I was a major photo op. I picked up my saddle and tried to find another spot but they followed me all over that airport snapping pictures and yelling, "Cowboy, cowboy!"

I had a particularly good fourth of July one year. Just getting to all the rodeos I wanted to during that Cowboy Christmas period was always a challenge. There's always a lot of planning and making travel arrangements, which most rodeo fans aren't aware is a critical part of what we do. That year I flew commercial to Denver, then rented a car there and drove to Greeley, where I rode that afternoon. I won fourth-place money there. I got back in the car, drove back to Denver and caught another flight, this time to Portland. I worked two rodeos out there, Molalla and St. Paul, and won them both. That was one of the better single days I ever had, winning two rodeos and placing at the other in a space of a little over twelve hours.

The fourth of July wasn't always that good to me. One year we started out from Springdale, Arkansas. We flew to Phoenix, rented a car and drove out to Prescott, Arizona. It was 120 degrees Fahrenheit that day. I got bucked off my horse there. We jumped back in the car and had to be in Window Rock up in Four Corners country that night. We thought we'd found a short cut but the map didn't tell us the road we were on was a maze of switchbacks through the mountains. All along the way there were little lakes and people out with their barbecues just enjoying the holiday. Here I was sweaty and sore from getting thrown off and not in a real good mood. It was all I could do to keep from pulling over and jumping into one of those lakes to cool off.

We barely made Window Rock in time but it didn't matter because I didn't make any money there either. Then it was back in the car and we drove all night to get back to Phoenix to catch a plane to get up to Calgary for the Stampede. That was another one of those chapters in the glamorous life of the rodeo cowboy.

CHAPTER 6

Glory Days

Sometimes, after all the miles, all the pain, all the disappointment

and all the money spent chasing the dream . . . well, sometimes

the dream comes true. And they win. And sometimes there are

victories every bit as important as the ones that result in

championships. Those victories are won in the arena of life.

* MONICA *

If I think of glory days in terms of rodeos I've won, I guess Denver is right up there. I won it in 1999 and to tell the truth, I was probably the most surprised person in the building when I did. I'd already won Rodeo Royal in Calgary earlier that spring and I felt really good about the way Giz was working but *this was Denver!*

I'd gone down there with Joan Unger and Randa. After my first two runs, everybody was telling me I'd made the Finals and that I might as well just stay until the last day. But I felt it would be better to take Giz home for the week between my second run and the short go. I wanted him in his own barn where he'd be comfortable and relaxed. And, most of all, I wanted him to be able to breathe.

Despite Denver's reputation as one of the great rodeos, the stabling conditions there are unbelievably bad. Most of us are in one giant barn. There are so many horses in there and no ventilation, it's terrible. Horses are forever getting sick at that rodeo.

For some reason they insist on keeping the doors closed at all times. Anybody going into that barn after it's been closed for a few hours is guaranteed burning and running eyes. Whenever any of the barrel racers go in or out of the place, we leave the door open but within seconds a guard rushes over to close it again. One year, some of us bribed a guy to let us stable our horses along one wall. A couple of people climbed up the wall and propped sticks in the windows to keep them open. It's sad that hauling a horse several hundred miles home and back is preferable to stabling right there at the rodeo. It's even sadder that one of the biggest rodeos in the world allows that to happen.

Bob went back down with me for the Finals. There were ten girls who had made it back to the Finals and on the last day they run from slowest to fastest based on the times on the first two runs. I came into the Finals in third place so I would be the third last to run. I knew there were two very good girls who would run after me. I tried to do what I always do, which is to concentrate hard on what I'm going to do and put the rest of it out of my mind.

Giz ran really well but we weren't perfect. We bowed a little coming off the last barrel but he ran hard and I knew we'd been pretty good. It was Bob who came out into the back area and told me I'd won. I didn't believe him, and I kept looking over my shoulder waiting for an official to come and tell me there was a mistake and I hadn't won after all.

But sure enough, I took the victory lap, received a gift certificate for a pair of ostrich boots and won over $10,000. And that did feel good. Even with the lousy stabling conditions, it was still Denver and still a great rodeo and certainly the biggest win of my career so far.

I'd be lying if I said helping to get the $50,000 for the barrel racers at the Calgary Stampede wasn't one of the things I'm proudest of. From the time I first became the Barrel Racing Director on the Board of the Canadian Professional Rodeo Association, I had been asking the Calgary Stampede to have us run for fifty thousand like the cowboys had been doing in their events since 1982. Finally, in 1996, Stampede officials told us that if we wanted to run for $50,000, we'd have to find a sponsor willing to put up $75,000 — fifty for the prize money and twenty-five for the Stampede's administration of the event.

That was the one thing I didn't want to do. I'd sworn when I was elected to the CPRA Board that under no circumstances would I ask people for money. That's just not something I'm comfortable doing.

But if that was the only way it was going to get done, I decided I would do what I could. Three people were extremely helpful in making it happen. One was Larry Evans, a Calgary businessman who pretty much guided me through the process of getting the money and even formed a company to handle the money for us.

The second was J.P. Veitch, bull rider and stockbroker. He took me to the Stampede's annual chuckwagon tarp auction, which is a huge fundraiser for the chuckwagon drivers. There are a lot of big companies and high rollers at that event. J.P. positioned us at the door so that he could introduce me to everyone as they came into the room where the auction was being held. By the end of the evening, I had secured the last twenty-five thousand we needed. The only problem was that it was in the form of three $25,000 chunks. As it turned out, when we met with Stampede officials, they weren't happy about having three different sponsors for the Barrel Racing and made arrangements for Purolator Courier to be the sole sponsor.

Larry took the additional $25,000 and put it toward the prize money at the Canadian Finals Rodeo. I'm not sure the cowboys ever realized that some of the money they won that year was courtesy of the barrel racers. One of the ways he used the money was to designate one event each night of the Finals, and the contestant from that event getting the biggest cheer would receive $1,500 — a thousand-dollar bill and five one hundreds. Friday night was Barrel Racing night and I had been racking my brain trying to come with some way of winning that money. Finally I had an idea. I was sitting on the stands early in the rodeo. Randa was sitting in the same row but down a ways from me. There were four women between us. I'm not sure what they thought of the conversation they heard that night between mother and twenty-year-old daughter.

Me: Are you wearing panties?

Randa: (Making a face) Yes.

Me: Are they coloured?

Randa: (Another face) Yes.

Me: Can I have them?

Randa: No way.

Me: I'll give you one hundred dollars.

Randa: No.

Me: Please.

Randa: Five hundred.

Me: Two-fifty.

Randa: Okay.

She didn't know what I wanted them for but sure enough I got the panties — they were red lace. Next I bribed Ponoka rodeo man Frank Mickey $100 to make sure the panties got picked up after I had done what I was planning with them. With the money I had invested, I either had to win the fifteen hundred or be out a fair chunk of money.

That night, as Giz and I ran home during our run in the Barrel Race, I pulled the red panties out from under the horn of my saddle and threw them into the air. I finished the run and Frank, true to his word, retrieved the underwear. Well, actually he *arranged* to have them retrieved. He sent an unsuspecting Denny Robbie out to collect the panties. Denny hadn't seen what happened and ran out there to pick up something red from the centre of the arena. When he got there, he realized what it was he was gathering up but by then it was too late. He picked up the panties and tried to hide them behind his back as he hurried back to the chutes.

I won the fifteen hundred. My friend Larry Evans came down to present me with the money and I presented him with the panties. There were a lot of sore stomachs from all the laughing that took place that night.

As much as I had dreaded the idea of having to find the $50,000 for the barrel racers, I have to say the experience was actually fun. It was certainly educational. There were so many highs and lows. I kept getting different deadlines from the

Stampede, which really put the pressure on. I was very upset during Rodeo Royal [Calgary's spring rodeo] because I knew I was running out of time to find the last twenty-five thousand. To make it worse, one Stampede official was saying I had three days to get the money, while another person was telling me it was already too late and to forget it.

Thank goodness for Stampede director, Rod McBride. He was with us right from the start and was instrumental in our getting a shot at the $50,000. I'm not sure the thing would have got done if it hadn't been for Rod's support.

Once we had the money, the next big obstacle was to have us as part of the Sunday Finals, which is when all the $50,000 events are run. At one point we were told there just wasn't time to fit us into the program. I pointed out that there would be lots of time if the Stampede simply moved the finals of the Novice Bareback and Novice Saddle Bronc events (they aren't $50,000 events) from Sunday to Saturday and moved us from Saturday to Sunday. Although my suggestion seemed to blow some minds at first, eventually that's exactly what happened. Finally women and men were equal partners at the Calgary Stampede.

With the equal money in place for the girls at Calgary, that left one other even bigger challenge — that was to get us equal money at the Canadian Finals Rodeo. The resistance there was such that all of us knew that only drastic measures would make it happen. The drastic measure turned out to be a letter that was sent to the Canadian Professional Rodeo Association in 1996 with copies to the prime minister; the premiers of Alberta, Saskatchewan and British Columbia; the editors of all the major daily newspapers, as well as most professional and amateur sports organizations.

Kelly at Cloverdale in 1998. (KIRBY MESTON)

Kelly at the 1997 Canadian Finals Rodeo. (KIRBY MESTON)

PREVIOUS SPREAD: Kelly Armstrong on Homer Simpson at the 1997 Stampede. Kelly is in the blue shirt he wears in honour of his great grandfather, George, who competed in every event at the first Calgary Stampede in 1912. (KIRBY MESTON)

Kelly makes a spectacular, though untraditional, entrance to the Canadian Finals Rodeo in 1997 — "The damned Harley almost bucked me off!" (KIRBY MESTON)

FOLLOWING SPREAD: Kelly in the first "go" at the 1992 National High School Rodeo Finals in Shawnee, Oklahoma. (JAMES FAIN)

Kelly rides to the championship at the 1998 Ponoka Stampede on Baird and Shellenburg's Cattlemen's Q91. (MIKE COPEMAN)

The results of that effort surprised a lot of people. Almost everyone who received the letter, especially the political figures, wrote and phoned the CPRA asking why these women didn't have equality at the Canadian Finals Rodeo. Ralph Murray, who was the general manager of the CPRA at the time, said at a directors' meeting, "I think it's about time we gave these girls what they're asking for. I can't think of any more excuses to give people about why they shouldn't be treated equally." It was Duane Daines who came up with a way to cut the pie so that the cowboys actually got a raise, although not as big a raise as they would have received had we not got equal money. Because the cowboys got more than they had been getting previously, it didn't bother them (or maybe they just didn't know) that we were now getting the same money as them.

There's no doubt that getting equal money for barrel racers was a big part of why I won the Guy Weadick Award at the Calgary Stampede and later the Cowboy of the Year for Canadian rodeo. The Guy Weadick is an award named after the founder of the Stampede. It is given each year to a person who exemplifies what Guy Weadick stood for. Mostly it is awarded to someone who presents himself or herself in a way that represents the positive qualities of our western heritage.

The Cowboy of the Year Award is similar in the criteria it is based on but it rewards the whole rodeo season and is presented at the Champion's banquet at the Canadian Finals Rodeo. People kid me about being the "Cowboy" of the Year but really the name of the award doesn't bother me and, to be honest, I don't think a name change needs to be a big priority. I'm just really proud to be the first woman to win either of those awards.

I received one other award that was an even bigger surprise than the other two. In 1997 I was named one of Alberta's ten

"Women on the Move." I was invited to a luncheon with the other honorees — there was a doctor, a lawyer and some business people there, a real cross-section of dynamic women. I was thrilled to be included in a group like that.

The luncheon was at La Caille on the Bow, a lovely Calgary restaurant, and I received a beautiful framed photograph of the fireworks at the Calgary Stampede. I thought that was fitting since at least part of why I was there, I'm sure, had to do with getting the fifty thousand for barrel racers at the Stampede. And there had been a few fireworks.

During the luncheon, the doctor leaned over to me and told me she had been named to some board that consisted entirely of male doctors and her. She asked if I had any advice for dealing with male-dominated groups. I told her that if she really wanted the group to do something, her best bet was to get the man sitting next to her to suggest it. I also told her that if she wanted something badly but it looked like she was going to lose, to retreat and try again another day.

I'm the last person I would think of as an activist. I don't like confrontation and mostly what I want to do is ride my horse. Barrel racing is all the excitement I really need. But there were things that had to be fixed and it looked like nobody else was going to fix them. I felt I had to try.

❋ K E L L Y ❋

I'm often asked what I feel was the best ride I ever made. I never hesitate when I'm asked that — I'm convinced my best ride ever was at Omak, Washington, in 1997. Of course, when I say that, the next thing people want to know is how many points I scored on that ride. I tell them 75. Right away they get that "Boy, you must really suck" look in their eyes. But it goes back to something I've thought about often and that is the personal fulfilment of knowing I've done my best.

This was a bull I did not want to have anything to do with. Nobody did. I didn't even want to go to that rodeo but it was later in the year, in August, and I said to myself, "I guess we'll find out how bad you want to go to the NFR." So I showed up in Omak and got on the bull. He turned back and spun hard — had a great day, a rideable day — but definitely not a day off for the rider. I got 75 points. Didn't win a dime.

Austin was standing next to Scott Breding, and the two of them were watching the ride. Neither could believe I actually rode the bull (any more than I could) and when I got off, Scott turned to Austin and said, "We just saw a 90-point bull ride." Scott is an NFR bull rider and he's won the $50,000 at Calgary. I'd say he has a pretty good eye for a quality bull ride and he thought it was great. Austin thought the same thing and so did I but the score was announced as 77 points.

Austin was positive there had to be some mistake. And there was. When he went to the rodeo office to check the judges' score cards, he discovered they had lowered the mark to 75. Obviously I would have liked more points but the men who get paid to judge saw it as a 75. And as far as I'm concerned that's what it was. What was more important than the score was the confidence boost that ride gave me. In fact, I was feeling so good about things that the next day I went to Lethbridge and got on the Kesler bull Excalibur. I'd been on that big black sucker three times before and he'd beat on me, chewed me up and spit me out all three times.

I hadn't been planning on going to Lethbridge. I figured why go there just so Excalibur could do a number on me all over again. But after Omak, I accepted this ride as a personal challenge. I told myself that if I did make it to the NFR, I'd see bulls there that tough and tougher. So I went over there and got on him and it went all right. Well, maybe better than all right. I was 84 points and won second. By that time my hat was starting to get a little tight, I was so high on myself. The next day we went to Cranbrook where I'd drawn Crocodile Rock, a bull I'd had before at Ponoka. I got along fine with him the previous time and I was thinking that after Excalibur, this was going to be a day at the beach.

But Crocodile Rock didn't see it that way. He whipped me down, smacked me in the face and broke off eight teeth (mine not his) in the back of my mouth. I travelled back to Calgary with calf roper Mark Nugent, and I spent the whole time in his trailer with a bag of frozen peas for an ice pack and a frozen water bottle for a pillow.

(Jeez, for a chapter on all my best moments in rodeo, this hasn't been a lot of fun so far.)

If I was to choose two rodeos that stand above all the rest in my memory so far, I'd pick Ponoka, Alberta, and Pendleton, Oregon, both in 1998.

Ponoka is one of Canada's oldest and best rodeos, and I always look forward to going there on the July 1 weekend. For my first bull I'd drawn a good one, C N Stars, from the Northcott Rodeo Company. I'd had him a couple of times before and I was tickled to have him again. But when I got to Ponoka, it was pouring so hard only Noah could have felt comfortable there. The arena was a swamp and I thought to myself, "Why today?" When I have a bull like that at a rodeo like that, I kind of like the weather to be decent. I remember back to when I was a kid riding steers, if it was raining hard when I was getting on, I wasn't as hungry to do well. There was more of a tendency to feel "Let's just get this over with and get somewhere dry."

I've realized since that there's a lot of money to be won in the rain, but I still wouldn't have minded a better day for that ride at Ponoka. I didn't bother putting on my chaps, I didn't even resin my rope; I didn't think either would do any good. I waited as long as I could to put my rope on him to try to keep it at least a little dry. With one guy left to go before me, I got ready real fast and when it was my turn I nodded and we got out of there in a hurry.

The bull was great. He bucked the same way he would have on dry ground. I wound up winning the go-round and having the lead going into the short round the next day. For the short go, I drew Cattlemen's Q91, a bull that's owned by Bob Baird and Rod Shellenberg. He's one of the premier bulls in Canada. I couldn't have scripted it any better, and to top things off the sun was trying to come out. I figured things were shaping up for one of those storybook endings.

Then just a few minutes before the Bull Riding, the rain picked up where it left off the day before, except that, if anything, it was coming down harder. That storybook was starting to look more like a Stephen King novel. I was the last guy to go and everybody else had been bucked off. In fact, that made two years in a row that no bull had been ridden in the short round at Ponoka.

Q91 was outstanding that day, like he is most days. And damn if I didn't ride him. Those aluminum grandstands at Ponoka were really rocking. I was 89 points to win the rodeo. When I went up to the podium to collect my buckle, I was asked what I thought of the 89 points I'd been given. I said I'd have been happy with a score of two — one for the bull and one for me. I took my first-place cheque from Ponoka and made my first land payment with it. I think doing something like that with the money made my win at Ponoka even more special.

Later that same year I went to the Pendleton Roundup down in Oregon. It's one of the great rodeos in North America, but it turned out to be even better than usual for me that September of '98. The first bull I got on there was pretty common. I'd had him earlier in the year and I was only 76 on him so I wasn't expecting a whole bunch from him. He bucked a little better at Pendleton, though, and I was 80. That was good enough to get me into the short round where I drew Jimmy Diesel, an awfully good bull of Canadian contractor Harvey Northcott.

Before the rodeo that day, I was walking through the camp where all the stock contractors stay during the week. I ran into Joe Baumgartner, the bullfighter, who was looking at the list of who had what in the Finals. Joe asked me how many bull riders I thought would ride their bulls. I said, "All of them."

Harvey happened to overhear our conversation and he laughed and said, "I know one who isn't gonna stay on today."

Harv and I hadn't seen eye to eye for quite some time, so it didn't surprise me any that he'd be betting against me. Actually, Jimmy Diesel was just coming back after being off for a year and a half with a broken leg. I'd seen him the week before at Armstrong, B.C., and he sure didn't show any ill effects from the injury. He was sensational there.

"Don't ever bet on black, Harv," was all I said to him. I'd heard that line in Vegas once and I thought it kind of fit the situation.

I went into the short round in fifth place so I was sitting in a decent spot. The bull bucked real good that day. He spun to the left just out of the gate, and at about five seconds he started back to the right. When I got off him, Flint Rasmussen, the rodeo clown, ran over to me and said, "You gotta throw your hat."

"No, I don't," I told him. "I'm not much of a hat thrower."

"Fine," Flint said and grabbed my hat off my head and threw it into the air just as the announcer gave my score as 81 points.

I was disappointed to hear that, but I shrugged my shoulders and went to get my hat. The announcer came back on the microphone a few seconds later to say there had been a mistake in adding up the judges' scores. My mark was actually 91 points. For a few seconds I couldn't believe what I'd heard. Everybody I know would like to win the Pendleton Roundup and I'd just done it.

They don't fool around when you win Pendleton. They presented me with an unreal amount of stuff: a saddle, a buckle, a watch, a hat, a jacket and a pair of boots. They had the saddle I had won already on a horse and the tradition there is for the winner to get on the horse and take a victory lap around the racetrack. There were probably fifteen thousand people there that day — they sell the thing out a year ahead. And the whole time I was riding around the track, the people in the stands were screaming. Then when I finished my victory lap, the organizers hustled me back over to the grandstand for still more presentations.

It's a scenario that everyone in this game dreams about. I had the best bull at the rodeo, I rode him for 91 points and a grandstand full of people loved me. I guess you'd call that "the thrill of the ride." Days like I had in Ponoka and Pendleton — those are the days when I love being a bull rider, they're what cowboys live for. They're also the days I lean on when that other kind of day comes along.

More than all the buckles and the trophies, one of my best moments in rodeo is one that only two people know about — my dad and me. Dad quit rodeo when he was still young to do the responsible thing and take care of his family. I know he lives vicariously through me but he's never put pressure on me. I put pressure on myself because I want my parents to be proud of me. That's a good pressure because it comes from me.

My dad has never said "Good ride" to me in all the years I've rodeoed. It's just not the way we do things in our family. But I remember one time at a little bull riding when I was about fifteen, I made a pretty good ride. When I got back to the chute, my dad shook my hand, smiled at me and winked. That's all it took. That moment meant a lot to me, more than any championship ever could.

Another real good day for me was March 11, 2000. That was the day I married my college sweetheart, Robyn. Maybe the best part of my education experience was meeting Robyn. My agriculture prof, Dr. Gary Don Harkey, was friends with the Byars family of Vernon and suggested I call their daughter Robyn and ask her out. I don't know how many students have professors who double as their dating coordinator.

But even with the advice of my instructor, I needed a little extra push. One of my roommates was Kirby Berry, a bareback rider from Weatherford, Texas. He happened to see the phone number lying on my desk and said, "What's this?" I told him it was the number of a girl named Robyn Byars but that I wasn't sure I was going to call her. He said he knew Robyn and told me she was a terrific girl. He wanted me to sit down and call her right then. It sure seemed a lot of people were working hard at getting this romance off the ground.

Anyway, I called her. It was one of those sweaty palm deals but it went okay and we went out. One of the first things I learned about Robyn was that she was quiet. Well, quiet is an understatement. Whenever I phoned her, before I dialled her number I wrote down some things to talk about. You talk about a bad interview — it was all one-word answers. The thing is, I don't know what happened but somewhere along the way she changed. Now I can't shut her up. I think I liked her better the old way. Jeez, if I could only turn back time.

I guess I should admit right here and now that once Robyn got into college — she started a year after we started going out — she pretty well carried me the rest of the way, especially those last months of my college career when I was AWOL trying to make the NFR.

We had a really nice wedding in Vernon and then a dance up in my hometown (now *our* hometown) of Big Valley a couple of weeks later. That way our friends on both sides of the border got to be with us and we really enjoyed both of those days. We'll be living in Big Valley but I know we're going to spend quite a bit of time in Texas as well. The Byarses are wonderful people, and they've made me feel welcome in their family. But there were a few days they must have wondered what they were getting for a son-in-law. I've pulled some of the same klutzy stuff at their place that used to drive my dad nuts. One time I folded up their satellite dish like a taco with the horse trailer. That's probably not the best way to impress the future in-laws.

Robyn and I have talked about it, and I don't see my rodeo life changing that much. She's a barrel racer and comes from a rodeo family so it's not like this is all new to her. She understands that I'm going to be away some of the time, and she's very independent. She wants to work with her horses and plans to rodeo in Canada.

And there will be times when we'll be able to rodeo together. I know it will mean a lot to me having the person I care most about in the stands cheering me on.

I'm a lucky guy and I know that. I have a beautiful wife I enjoy being with. But even better, we have many of the same goals and dreams for the rest of our lives. And that should make for a whole lot of glory days for the two of us.

✳ DUANE ✳

The years 1989 to 1993 were probably my best in rodeo. It was during that time that I think I had just the right combination of youthful energy and the experience that comes from doing something for a long time. The years before that I had been learning how to ride in the big leagues. But during that five-year stretch from '89 to '93 I learned how to win. I think it's a lot like other sports where experience and the ability not to make mistakes are what makes winners. I remember teasing the Hay boys, Rod and Denny, when they were rookies in '89 that they could ride better than me but I knew how to win better than they did.

During that stretch I was fortunate to enjoy some mighty successful moments. But I've always felt that consistency is the real mark of excellence in anything we do in life. And qualifying for the National Finals Rodeo nine times, including every one of those years between 1989 and 1993, was one of the things I'm proudest of.

Championships are important to any cowboy, especially one as competitive as I am. I'm proud that I won Houston twice and the All-Around at San Antonio — that got me a pickup truck — and the Bronc Riding at Fort Worth. And, of course, winning the Canadian All-Around Championship three times meant a lot to me. But a lot of the time, what I felt after winning those championships was relief. I think that's often the case when athletes chase a dream for a long time and begin to wonder if they'll ever get there.

That's certainly the way it was with me and the Canadian Saddle Bronc Riding title. I'd been chasing that son-of-a-gun for a long time and getting more and more frustrated at not winning the thing. I'd been the season leader three different times and I'd been close to winning the title a few times but I just couldn't seem to get over the hump. I'd tell myself that everyone goes into the Finals on an equal footing and I should be able to win it but "should" doesn't cut it — I hadn't won. So when I did in 1991, I was a pretty happy guy.

I'd been having a good year and went to the Finals feeling healthy and confident. The week started out with several of us winning a little but nobody getting too far out in front of the pack. After three performances, it was still a close race. It was Saturday that really got it done for me. That's a critical day anyway with two performances. With 40 points for a first, 30 for second, 20 for third and 10 for fourth in each round, a competitor can do some serious damage if he rides well that day. And if a guy sleeps through Saturday, most of the time he can kiss his chances goodbye.

I drew two real good horses that day and won the afternoon round, which gave me a little cushion. It didn't hurt to know that I had Bar T Bay for the evening performance. The horse belonged to Donnie Pederson, and I'd had him for my first horse the year before in the $50,000 round at Calgary. He'd been good with me then, and I was hoping for more of the same.

Sure enough, he was outstanding that night in Edmonton, and I got along with him pretty well. I won the round, which along with my win in the afternoon, gave me 80 points for the day and clinched the Bronc Riding championship for me. The funny thing is I didn't realize it right away. I was concentrating so hard on just making a good ride on a good horse I hadn't really been doing the math. But when the other guys started coming up and congratulating me, it sunk in that I'd just accomplished something I'd wanted to for a very long time. It was a tremendous feeling.

The week ended on a bit of a sour note though. I had already clinched the All-Around title as well for the second time in my career. But there was one other championship I had a shot at — the High-Point Award. That goes to the guy winning the most money over the season in any two or more events. It was down to Joe Lucas and me. Joe is an outstanding calf-roper who's won lots of championships. He also bulldogs some steers, which is what made him eligible for the High-Point.

I had the Calgary Stampede horse Papa Smurf, one of the greatest horses of all time and the best horse in the draw that day. Joe was so sure I'd win the High-Point, he left after he'd competed. And I would have won it too if I hadn't screwed up. I made a great ride on him but I missed him out at the gate. The judges hadn't called it all week but they had nailed another guy two ahead of me. I should have realized I'd have to be careful because a lot of times if they get one guy they like to get two.

I missed the horse out, there's no doubt in my mind about that. But after they called the first spur out, I should have known I had to bear down and not make any mental mistakes because that was the only thing that could beat me. I made one and it did beat me.

Still it didn't break my heart all that much. I'd won two of the three titles I had a shot at, and especially winning that Bronc Riding put me on top of the world. It was great in the dressing room after it was over. I could tell the guys were really happy for me. They'd been trying to beat me all week, but when it was over they were pleased for me just like I'd been pleased for other guys when they'd won it.

Being the Saddle Bronc Riding Champion of Canada didn't change my life all that much. I was the champ for about two weeks, and then it was time to start all over again. The slate was clean; I was off to the next rodeo. I think it was later that I realized how important it was to win a championship like that. I relate it to other sports and a guy like John Elway, who everybody wanted to win that Super Bowl, which he did. Or a Dan Marino, who didn't. Or a Ray Bourque in hockey with so many people wanting him to get his name on that cup.

So it is important. You're in the record books and no one can ever take it away from you. Now that my career is over, I think it's more meaningful than ever that I was able to get that title. I don't think I'd have been devastated if I hadn't won. I think the only thing I would have regretted would have been knowing that I hadn't tried as hard as I could have all those years. And I know I gave everything I had year after year. Still, when all is said and done, I'm glad I was the Bronc Riding Champion of Canada in 1991.

For a single moment that stands out during a long career, winning the $50,000 at the Calgary Stampede was pretty exceptional. You're having a real good day when that happens. The Stampede and Houston have always been my favourite rodeos, and with Calgary so close to home it's kind of like my hometown rodeo. Up to that year — 1990 — no Canadian bronc rider had ever won the $50,000 prize on that last day of the Stampede. One of the Calgary newspaper guys called me wanting to write a "me against the world" story. I told him it really wasn't that way, but in fact it was.

That year there were ten guys who had qualified for the final Sunday. Five came through the first nine days of the Stampede, the others through the Budweiser Series that used to get five guys into the $50,000 round. The other nine finalists were Americans. I was trying not to think about that. The top four scores from the ten finalists would move on to the Final Four and get on another horse. The top mark on two would be the $50,000 winner.

I just wanted to ride my first one good enough to get me into the Final Four. I'd been to the $50,000 round before so I kind of knew what to expect. I had my oldest daughter, Jennifer, with me. She was only four, but she could sense something big was happening that morning because a lot of guys were wishing me well in the coffee shop. She told me to try real hard. I promised her I would.

One thing I'd learned the other times I'd been there was to really go for it on the first horse. I think a lot of times the thing is won on that first ride even though it's the total points on two that determines the champ. I'd drawn my old friend Bar T Bay for my first one. He was great, and I was leading with a little cushion after the round of ten. Being the leader going into the Final Four is a good spot to be in because you get to watch the other guys go before you.

Because of ties, six guys actually earned a second horse that afternoon. In the Final, Lewis Feild, an outstanding bronc rider, was making a terrific ride on a great Calgary horse, Lonesome Me, but he bucked off right at the whistle. I'm pretty sure if he'd made it the full eight seconds, the thing would have been his. After Lewis bucked off, I realized that if I didn't screw up I could win it. That's when the pressure really set in. I kept telling myself, "Get a good spur-out and don't make any mistakes." Of course, that's when you often make a mistake just as I did a year later in the final round at the CFR.

While I watched the other five guys ride, I could feel myself getting pretty hyped up. I kept telling myself I had the lead and that I'd drawn a good horse for my Final Four ride. *Just go out there and do what you've done a thousand times before.* My second horse was a Calgary bronc named Ms Rocket. She wasn't originally in the draw for the Final Four but got in when they needed six horses.

She's a nice mare and I was happy to have her. I got a good spur-out on her but then she blew up on me and I was in a jam for a jump or two. For the first time in my career, I actually heard the crowd during that ride. There was a little home-field advantage there and that helped a bunch. I really cranked it up from that point on.

The ride ended and the pickup man, Wayne Vold, came in and set me down on the ground. Wayne had one finger in the air to indicate I had won it, the crowd was going nuts and rodeo announcer Dave Poulsen was into it pretty good too. As I hit the ground, I went through the ride quickly in my mind. I knew I'd finished strong and that I'd spurred better on my left side than my right.

I threw my hat in the air, which is something I just didn't do in my career. I didn't plan to do it then either, but there was just so much emotion happening. I thought with the lead I'd had coming in and the ride I'd made that it would be close but maybe I had enough to win it. But you never really know until you hear that score.

The score was announced and sure enough I'd won the fifty thousand dollars. I barely had time to get happy. Things happen pretty fast around there. I was still trying to catch my breath when someone grabbed my arm and started hustling me up to the stage for the presentation. People were slapping me on the back as I was running across the infield to the stage and it started to sink in that I'd done what I'd set out to do.

I was running as fast as chaps and spurs would let me when somebody pointed to where Jennifer was yelling and jumping up and down. Again it wasn't rehearsed but I grabbed her up in my arms and took her up on stage with me. They presented me with the cheque and I said something — I can't remember if it made sense or not — because the whole thing is pretty much a blur.

I did a bunch of interviews over beside the stage and then, just like that, the rodeo was over. The place was clearing out and I headed back across the infield to pick up my bronc saddle. I got back over behind the chutes and one of the committee people was setting things up for the chuckwagon races. I think we were about the only two people around there. He came over and congratulated me. It's funny, I didn't even know the guy, yet that was the moment when I was able to tell myself, "Hey, we did something today." I picked up that old bronc saddle I'd been partners with for a long time and walked out of there with a feeling inside that was awful good.

There have been some special moments outside the arena for me too. My family takes top spot. I met my wife, Cheryl, in 1991. I wasn't really looking for anybody at the time. I'd been divorced in 1990 from my first wife, Marla. We'd had two wonderful daughters, Jennifer and Bailey, and I was trying to spend as much time as I could with them. That, along with my rodeo schedule didn't leave much time for dating.

Cheryl had been around rodeo as Miss Rodeo Canada in 1987 and she barrel-raced so I knew who she was but I didn't know her well. We'd done some remotes on radio to promote different things a few times and I'd chatted with her then.

I still tease her that she was after me pretty good that summer of '91. She'd come by where I was parked pretending she needed to water her horse. I'd tell her she'd already watered him five times. The truth is when I got to a rodeo I was pretty busy, especially here in Canada, where I was roping and bronc riding. There was a lot to do to get ready for two events. I had a routine I liked to follow as a buildup to competing. There was the physical preparation — warming up my roping horse, then lots of stretching to get ready for my bronc. And I always felt that the mental preparation was important. I liked to have time to really focus on what I had to do at every rodeo. I didn't get to do much socializing.

Cheryl and I ran into each other again at a rodeo in Saskatoon. She just really impressed me as a nice person. When I got back home, I decided to phone her and ask her out. She'd just finished an education degree at university and was staying at her folks' place in Rimbey. I was like a high school kid, I was so nervous making that phone call. I asked her out for supper and she said yes.

Things went along pretty well after that. I even sold her my dually pickup. The next year she went with me to some of the winter rodeos. I won a pickup for the All-Around that year at San Antone and we drove back to Canada together. Her mom figured if we could stand each other for forty-five hours in the cab of that pickup, we should be all right together. When we were married in 1994, I felt I was the luckiest guy in the world. Plus I got my dually back.

We had our daughter, Sydney, in December 1995. The day Cheryl and I got married and the days my three daughters were born top my list in that "glory days" category.

* C H A P T E R * 7

Darkest Hours

Rodeo, like all professional sports, is not without its down side.

Certainly there is the agony of defeat but there are greater agonies

too. In a sport where danger is a very real part of every day in

the life of a competitor, serious injury and worse can and does

occur. And while no cowboy or cowgirl dwells on that aspect of

the sport, there is a grim awareness that heartbreak and tragedy

may be as near as the next ride, the next run or the next trip

down the road.

✳ **M O N I C A** ✳

I guess there are disappointing moments in anything that involves competition. One of my big ones was at the Stampede in 1999. By winning Rodeo Royal back in March, I'd won a bye into the top ten and the run for the $50,000 on the Final Stampede Sunday. I wasn't confident exactly, but I felt that we had a chance if things kind of went our way. But as we were in the box getting ready to make the run, Giz whirled around and I lost a stirrup. Some girls wear elastics on their feet to keep them in the stirrups but I'm not comfortable riding that way. I guess it cost me that day. I rode like a sack of potatoes and we didn't make it into the Final Four. That was disappointing for me, not because we didn't win but because I hadn't performed the way I wanted to.

But then I think about what I love about this sport. There's always another rodeo tomorrow. The next one might not be for $50,000 but at least it's a chance for me to do what I didn't do at the last one.

Barrel racers are often teased that we treat our horses better than we treat our husbands. I don't think it's quite that extreme but we do eat, sleep and breathe these horses, and when one of them is sick or dies, it's like losing part of ourselves. Anyone who is in this business long enough may have to face that situation at some point and it is the hardest part of what we do.

I've had two horses in my life that I would consider super. One is Giz. The other was Chicken. Chicken and I won the FCA together in 1985. Back then all my horses were turned out in a field and at night I called them in to be fed. One night Chicken just didn't eat, which was unusual for him and is never a good sign with any horse. I put him in a pen away from the other horses and watched him for a while. I took his temperature and it was 104 degrees. When I called the vet clinic at Okotoks, the vet said I better bring him in because 104 was pretty high.

I took him in and he got progressively worse for about three days. Finally they said he was coming around so I went and got him. I had him home for a couple of days and he got sick again. I took him back in and that time he was in there for over a week. While he was there the second time, I called a psychic, Karen Hamel. I know there are people who don't have much confidence in the advice of a horse psychic, but some of us have had amazing success with people like Karen. She told me over the phone that Chicken had Potomac fever and he should have a big dose of Banamene and Kaopectate. When I told the people at the vet clinic what she said, they told me they had given him Pepto-Bismol and that should do it. It didn't and after eight days and $2,700, Chicken died. The vet said it was salmonella poisoning and maybe it was.

Almost exactly a year later I put Pearce, who I was running at the time, in the same pen Chicken had been in. It was raining really hard that day and that pen had a shelter he could get into. Two weeks later we went to a rodeo in Val Marie, Saskatchewan. After the barrel race I tied Pearce to the trailer to give him his grain. He usually loved his grain but that day he didn't want anything to do with it. Pretty soon he was showing all the same signs Chicken had.

Suddenly he had diarrhea, and it just shot out of him about ten feet straight back. I was getting really worried so I called Karen again. She told me my horse was in major trouble, that everything inside of him had shut down and to get him to a vet as fast as I could. I raced off to the vet in Brooks. He had saved another barrel racer's horse the year before and I thought if anybody should see

Pearce it was him. We got there at four o'clock in the morning. The vet didn't know what was wrong but right off he gave Pearce a huge dose of Banamene and Kaopectate. The horse was at that clinic for ten days. My bill was $127 and he lived.

I'm convinced that whatever Chicken died of, this horse got from being in the same pen even though it was a year later. I've never kept a horse in that pen since. I store hay in it instead.

During the latter part of the 1999 season and into 2000, I had to face the possibility that Giz's career may be over. I can honestly say it's one of the roughest things I've ever had to deal with.

Giz was only fifteen in 1999, not that old for a barrel horse. I've had him longer and been more places on him than any horse I've ever owned. He's more than the horse I compete on. He really is one of the family (but not more important than my husband!). We've had so much success together. In addition to Denver, Rapid City and San Angelo in the States, here in Canada we've won Wainwright and Grande Prairie three times each; we won Falkland, Leduc, Swift Current — where we hold the arena record — and, of course we've qualified for eight Canadian Finals rodeos together.

And I was sure there were lots more wins in Giz. But during the summer of '99 we were running at Dawson Creek. As we were going into the first barrel, Giz overextended one front leg and almost went down. I felt right away that something was wrong. The vets checked him over and said he'd torn the tendons in that leg. They didn't know if he'd come back from that or not — they said it could go either way. But he did come back, about a month before the Canadian Finals Rodeo. They did an ultrasound on him and said he was fully recovered from the injury.

I started legging him up for the Finals, but about a week after I started riding him he got sick, really sick. He wouldn't eat and I knew something major was wrong. The vets did all kinds of tests on him and every test they did came out bad. His white blood cell count was way up and his red cell count was really low. They started him on different medications and I worked on getting him to eat. I kept pouring the hay to him because he would actually eat it, and he developed laminitis, also called founder, a foot ailment that's often related to eating. Eating too much of the hay along with being in a stall and not getting much exercise might have contributed to it.

On top of that, he got an infection in the coffin joint in one hoof. The vets injected him for that and we put shoes on him that were supposed to help with that problem. He got lamer and lamer until finally I pulled the shoes off him. As soon he got those shoes off, he started walking better but he was still lame.

All those things happening right together like that took a toll on Giz. I saw four vets and the news was mostly bad. It looked like he'd never be sound again. I put him in his own little pasture out at our place and decided to give him all the time he needed to recover. I figured if it took a year or even two years, that would be okay. And if he never made it back, he'd spend the rest of his life out there in retirement.

I always think things happen for a reason. I really liked my new horse, Ace, and thought that maybe Giz was hurt because I was supposed to go on with Ace. There are always other horses but that doesn't make it any easier to say goodbye to a friend. I'm sure it's that way in team sports when someone retires. The other people on that team feel bad about losing that teammate. Well, Giz was my teammate and I knew I was going to miss him.

When he was young, I always said I can't wait till he's older because he's going to be awesome as a twelve- or thirteen-year-old. And he was. In 1998 and '99 we were hard to beat, especially in the first half of the season. It's just been the last few years that he has become a truly great horse. I really thought with the way he's built and not having a hard life at all that he'd go until he was twenty or more. And I felt that he'd just keep getting better and better. I was really looking forward to the 2000 season and beyond just knowing how much better he was going to be. When it wasn't looking like that would happen I felt terrible. I was disappointed for him, and for me too, because I wouldn't have my friend in the trailer when I was going down the road and I wouldn't have him running his heart out for me.

But late in the spring of 2000, Giz started looking better. I could tell just by watching him that he felt better too. He's still out there in that pasture because I'm afraid to rush him. It was tempting to throw a halter on him and pony him around behind another horse just to see what he could do. But I didn't.

Giz doesn't owe me a thing. For all the trouble we had when I first got him, he's been wonderful. In 1999 he won the award the barrel racers call "Horse With the Most Heart." That award pretty well sums up Dr. Gizmo perfectly. That's why I'm going to give him every chance I can to come back. And I do believe that he will come back.

✳ KELLY ✳

Nineteen ninety-eight had been a real good year. I qualified for both the Canadian Finals and the National Finals rodeos. I was riding better than I ever had, cashing cheques almost everywhere

I went and I started to believe that it was just going to continue to be that way. My confidence, my belief in myself and my bank balance were at an all-time high. I guess I was like a lot of guys when that level of success comes — I started to think I was ten feet tall and invincible.

Then along came Mission Impossible. It was the final performance of the Canadian Finals and he was the last bull I'd be getting on before the NFR. I rode him fine but as I went to get off, my foot caught in my bull rope for a split second. It jerked my leg and I landed awkwardly. I'm positive the bull didn't step on me but it was one of those freak injuries that will happen maybe one time out of a million or so bull rides. I found out later that my knee was dislocated and three of the four ligaments in my knee were torn on impact with the ground.

The dislocation turned out to be the worst part of the injury and was what almost cost me my leg. Dale Butterwick, from the Pro Rodeo sports medicine team and the head athletic therapist for the University of Calgary, was quoted in the newspaper as saying it was the worst knee injury he'd seen in fifteen years of treating athletic injuries.

At the time I had no idea how bad I was hurt. I did know I was in a lot of pain. Bullfighters Ryan Byrne and T.J. Baird were the first people to get to me. Ryan said he thought my leg was broken but I said I thought it was my knee. The sports medicine guys, Dexter Nelson and Dale, got there right away and while they were checking me over, it felt like my knee sort of popped back in. Right then it felt a lot better. In fact, it felt so much better than what it had felt like before that I was sure I could walk out of there.

Dale wouldn't let me do that. "Just let us take you out of here, Kelly," he said, "and we'll take a look at it."

There was a doctor there as well but it was mostly Dale who was handling things. When they got me into the dressing room and got my pants off, Dale took one look and he didn't even say anything; he just turned and left the room. A few minutes later he came back and told me what he thought was wrong. I didn't really understand what he was talking about and I damn sure had no idea how bad this thing was. I remember thinking, "I'll have to learn how to tape my knee because the NFR starts in a few weeks."

Dale arranged an appointment with a couple of surgeons for the next morning. Austin and Robyn got me loaded up and we went to stay with my cousin, Jay Humphrey, who lives just outside of Calgary. The medical people had given me some pretty major painkillers and I needed them. We sat around at Jay's house talking for a while, and I decided I wanted to lie down. I got up on the crutches — there was just a little cardboard splint deal on my knee — and started for the bedroom. I took about five steps and started to feel dizzy. I stopped to get my bearings and the next thing I knew I was toppling into a bookcase and taking a nap.

The next morning I met with Dr. Mohtadi and Dr. Frank. Dr. Mohtadi told me I was lucky not to have lost my leg. They told me they couldn't operate for a few weeks until the swelling went down. But they didn't leave any doubt about the fact that they *would* be operating. About then it dawned on me that I wasn't likely to be going to the Finals in Vegas.

For the next few days, the phone never stopped ringing. A lot of people called who were really concerned about me. But in the middle of all the pain and disappointment and confusion I was feeling, T. J. Walter from the PRCA called Tuesday morning (I'd got hurt on Sunday), to find out whether I'd be going to the NFR or if I was drawing out. He said he needed to know right then. He called a few times. That made me mad. I was still trying to get my head around being hurt and here's a guy demanding I make a major decision on the spot. Talk about making a bad situation worse. If the pain hadn't already been keeping me awake at night, those phone calls from the PRCA would have.

After a couple of weeks, the pain had let up some and I could even walk a bit. The problem was that if I lifted my leg up in the air, the bottom half of it swung back and forth like a pendulum. I went to Texas to stay with Robyn and her family for Christmas, and my leg got to feeling good enough that I thought I'd like to try getting on a horse just to see if I could ride and squeeze with my legs. I even got to thinking that maybe I didn't need the surgery after all. But when I got home and met with the doctors again, they put a stop to that line of thinking in a hurry.

I was scared to death of having the surgery. I'd only spent one night in a hospital in my whole life and I wasn't real comfortable with the idea of being there now. But the morning of December 30, I headed for the Peter Lougheed Hospital in Calgary. I got there early for the big day — that wasn't by choice, they wanted me there early to get me ready.

They got me onto a rolling stretcher and prepared me for what was to come. The part that spooked me most was when they took me from a waiting room where there were some nurses and doctors into a different room where there was nobody. Lying there by myself, I got to having some pretty negative thoughts. Eventually the doors opened and they came for me. It seemed like the trip to the operating room took forever. I was starting to think we'd been up and down every corridor and hallway in the place.

When we finally got there, I saw one of my surgeons waiting for me just outside the operating room. He was wearing coveralls and rubber boots. I thought maybe they'd missed the operating room and wheeled me into the vet clinic. The doctor kidded me about that and then it was into the Operating Room, or the O.R. as they say on TV. People kept asking me which leg they were supposed to be operating on. I told them, "Maybe the one with no hair and a big X on it." I'm sure they were just doing that to lighten me up or maybe to see how with it I was but about the fifth or sixth time I got asked that question, I got a little concerned.

I couldn't believe how many people were in that operating room. There were doctors and nurses everywhere. Across the room my surgeon was cueing up the CD player. Then one of the nurses asked me if my chest was hurting. It was, and naturally I thought that was a bad thing. But I didn't get to worry about it for too long because the next thing I knew I was sleeping.

When the surgery was over and I was out of the anesthetic, they told me it would be a good idea for me to stay the night but that I didn't have to. I was out of there like a shot. That night I stayed at Jay's again. Robyn was with me, and she doesn't deal all that well with pain and blood — all that kind of stuff. But we got through that night and went home to Big Valley the next day. In the middle of that first night back at the house, I woke up in the night having to go to the bathroom. I was sleeping on the couch and Robyn was upstairs in my room. I got to the bathroom and got back as far as the kitchen when I started feeling dizzy again. I tried to prop myself up on the kitchen cupboard hoping it would pass but that didn't work. I wound up crashing backwards onto the floor out colder than a mackerel.

Robyn came running down the stairs thinking I'd been killed. I came to and was all right but that was the last time I took the painkillers. It was either that or start wearing a hockey helmet around the house.

After a month or so the doctors told me I could go to physio but not to overdo it — no more than once or twice a week. But I hounded the physiotherapist in Stettler to the point that she let me come every day. In fact, I think the people in that office were pretty much sick of me after a while. Eventually they told me I didn't need an appointment, I could just come whenever I wanted. I've never been a real fitness type, but I was never so motivated to work on an exercise program in my life.

It was rewarding because by September of '99 my injured knee was only twelve to fifteen per cent weaker than my other one. The doctor told me that given what I'd done to the knee, that was a pretty exceptional recovery. He told me that because I hadn't damaged it any further during rehabilitation, it was up to me to decide when I could start riding bulls again.

I got on a few practice bulls right after that and the knee felt fair at best. I knew it wasn't quite right. I was glad about one thing though. Getting on those bulls made me realize I hadn't forgotten how to ride. I felt so good about that I decided to just give the knee some more time before I came back full-time. And it was the weekend of the Canadian Finals Rodeo, exactly one year after I had been hurt, that I got back at it. I went to a Professional Bull Riders (PBR) Touring Pro Bull Riding in Florida and bucked off right out of the gate. I was thinking about the knee and not about riding that bull.

The next week I went to Wichita Falls, Texas. I got two re-rides and when I finally got a good bull, I was 90 in the long go and 86 in the short go later that same night. That convinced me that I was all right and that my knee was all right too. Of course there is still the possibility of re-injuring the knee. I don't know if it's any higher than with anyone else but I do know that if I hurt it again, there's a pretty good chance they won't be able to fix it.

I prefer to look at things more positively. My attitude after the injury healed up is that if that's the worst I'm ever going to get hurt in my career, I won't be doing too damn bad.

Bar none, the saddest and toughest day of my rodeo life was March 16, 1996. I don't believe that anything can ever happen that will affect me as much as the events of that day did.

I was in Camrose and had the bull Cattlemen's Q91, the same bull I would win Ponoka on two years later. I was first to go in that performance and he threw me off in a hurry. I was just hanging out behind the chutes helping some of the other guys get on. Lari Sluggett, a bull rider from Montana, was the next guy to ride. He had a bull named Tremors. The bull turned back right out of the chute and as he was being bucked off, Lari fell underneath the bull. The bull stepped on him, not out of any meanness but mostly because he couldn't help it. We see dozens of guys get stepped on out there and most of the time it's painful but not that serious.

I jumped over the back of the chute to help Lari out of the arena. The paramedics got there right away, and we unzipped Lari's vest to get him some air, thinking he just had the wind knocked out of him. Lari had travelled to that rodeo alone, so while the paramedics took him off on a stretcher, I gathered up his gear and told him we'd come by the hospital later to drop off his stuff and see how he was doing.

One of the ambulance attendants asked me if I wanted to go with him to the hospital. I decided I would, seeing as Lari didn't have anybody with him. I knew that if it was the other way around, he'd come with me. On the way to the hospital, I still had no idea that anything was seriously wrong.

When we got to the hospital, Lari was in the emergency area and they were giving him the sort of routine checks you'd expect. One of the reasons I didn't think his injuries could be very bad was that they let me stay with him. I stayed close by while they checked him over and we talked about his ride.

The pain seemed to be getting worse. I just kept reassuring him that everything was going to be fine. And I was still totally convinced of that although I noticed people were starting to move quicker and they were looking more solemn. All the time I was telling Lari that he was okay, he was shaking his head and saying no. Finally he asked me to phone his wife, Kate. I'd heard Lari speak of Kate but I'd never met her. He was able to give me the phone number at home and even the phone number of Kate's parents where she was staying that weekend. I figured it was a good sign that he was able to remember those numbers and communicate the information to me.

I called Kate and told her Lari had been stepped on and was here at the hospital but that everything seemed all right. I told her I didn't think it was any big deal but that Lari had wanted me to call her. Naturally she was worried, but I tried to reassure her the same way I'd been doing with Lari.

As I started back into the room Lari was in, the doctor pulled me off to one side and told me they had just called Stars Air Ambulance. They needed to get Lari to Edmonton in a hurry. It was going to be thirty-five or forty minutes before Stars could get there so I went back into the room to talk with him and just be there. That's when I first sensed that something was real wrong. The medical people told me they were going to take Lari to another room for some test they needed to do. As they were wheeling him out of the room, he said to me, "Tell Kate I love her."

I went out to phone Kate again to keep her updated, and when I came back, they had taken Lari out for the test.

When the doctor came out of the room from administering the test, I'd had about enough. He'd been putting me off to that point, and I wanted to know exactly where we were at. I got him cornered and told him I wanted to know what the hell was going on. He told me it didn't look very good at all.

When they brought Lari out of there, they put him in what looked like a yellow insulated sleeping bag. He'd been saying how cold he was and I think maybe the bag was to keep him warm. Stars arrived then and they loaded Lari up in a hurry and took off for Edmonton. Austin and a couple of other guys got to the hospital just after that. As we headed back to the rodeo grounds, I told them as much as I knew about what was going on. We got our stuff together, and Austin and I left for Edmonton which was about an hour away.

I talked to Kate two or three times as we drove into Edmonton. She was already in her vehicle and on her way to Edmonton from her parents' place in Wyoming. The last time I talked to her, she asked me to tell Lari the next time I saw him that she loved him.

When we got to the hospital, it was after midnight. We waited for a long time and finally it was like a scene from a movie when the doctors are coming down the hall looking real serious. They took us into a little room and closed the door. One of them said, "First off, he didn't make it."

Those words, when I heard them, didn't mean anything to me. This wasn't the way the story was supposed to end. I got mad and said, "I don't believe you. I want to see him."

They said they'd need a little time before that could happen and they left. It was maybe three-quarters of an hour later that they came

You can't ride 'em all! Duane leaves the back of Northcott's Wyatt Earp at the 1994 Canadian Finals Rodeo. (KIRBY MESTON)

FOLLOWING SPREAD: Duane catches one at the Calgary Stampede in 1990. (RAY JOHNSTON)

Duane makes a showy ride at the Calgary Stampede in 1991. (DAVID JENNINGS)

Duane and Cheryl get ready to load Cheryl's horse. (DAINES FAMILY COLLECTION)

PREVIOUS SPREAD: Duane at the Ponoka Stampede on the Calgary Stampede bronc Ms. Rocket. (KIRBY MESTON)

to get us. We put on all that hospital gear and started walking. I was in such a trance at that point, I can't remember whether we went upstairs, downstairs or stayed on the same floor. I do remember going down a hall that seemed three miles long. Finally we stopped and the doctor pointed and said, "He's right in there."

We went in and I stood there for a while, just trying to make myself understand everything that had happened that night. Finally I went over to Lari, kissed him on the forehead and told him Kate loved him.

Austin and I went back out into the hall and the place seemed deserted. There was nobody around. We started walking toward the waiting room and the phones. Suddenly a guy appeared from somewhere and said, "Hey, guys, you might want this." He handed me Lari's protective vest.

When we got to the waiting area, I phoned Kate and then Lari's parents. I reached Lari's dad and he told me Lari's mom had just left to meet Kate and travel up here with her. He said he'd try to catch the girls before they left for Canada.

When I got off the phone, the feeling I had was that everything was just so incredibly weird. There we were sitting in a hospital in Edmonton at four o'clock in the morning thinking, "What do we do now?" I'd gone to that hospital believing I would be leaving there with Lari. That wasn't going to happen and mostly I felt completely confused. What *do* you do at a moment like that?

That's when the thing about life going on kicks in. I was up at a rodeo in Medicine Hat later that day, and if I was going to get there in time we had to leave. We went back to the rodeo grounds in Camrose, picked up Lari's car and I drove that car to Medicine Hat. I went out to Mom and Dad's when I got to Medicine Hat and had a shower and cleaned up. Dad told me I didn't have to ride that night if I didn't want to, but I thought to myself, "If I don't ride today, I never will again."

I don't remember much about the rodeo. I stayed at home as long as I could, just puttering around. I went outside and looked at the cows and did a few chores. All the while what had happened over the previous twenty-four hours still seemed like a bad dream.

Dad and I went to the rodeo together. I didn't go into the building until about fifteen minutes before the Bull Riding. When I walked in there, it felt like everybody in the place stopped what they were doing and looked at me. I know they were feeling bad for me but that was really hard. I didn't want to look anybody in the eye; I just wanted to ride and get out of there.

I spent the next day at home. I took a lot of time getting all of Lari's stuff put away in his rigging bag the way he would have put it if he'd been able to. One of my bull riding buddies, Jeff Whitlow, came out to the house and we got in Lari's car and left for Lari's home in Montana. Driving into the yard of those people I'd never met with the stuff that belonged to their husband and son was one of the toughest things I've ever done in my life. And yet when they opened the door, it felt like I'd known them for a hundred years. Jeff and I stayed for a few days, went to Lari's funeral and eventually went back home.

One year later at Camrose, I drew the same bull, Tremors, Lari had ridden the night he was killed. I can't say I was afraid — he wasn't that bad a bull — but I sure did some thinking as I was getting on.

It was a long time before I could talk about the spring of 1996. It was something that will stay with me forever. Yet even out of that kind of tragedy, there was something good. I became friends with the Sluggetts, a wonderful rodeo family.

I still think a lot about Lari Sluggett and the person he was.

✳ DUANE ✳

Cheryl and I were married in 1994, and I decided I'd take it a little easy that year, especially during the summer. So instead of racing off after Calgary to Cheyenne and California, I made what we call the eastern run here in Canada. I went to Bengough and Kennedy and Estevan in Saskatchewan and Morris, Manitoba. I'd gone to Morris most years but usually I was there about an hour and gone. That summer I'd kidded people they'd be able to come by our trailer for a barbecue and a beer in Morris. And some of them did.

But when I saw the guys leaving there for Salinas and Cheyenne, I was itching to be going with them. It wasn't my style to be sitting around in a lawn chair relaxing when there were broncs to ride at some of the big rodeos.

So I wanted to get back after it pretty hard in '95. I'd been to the NFR five years in a row before my relaxation year in '94 and I was hoping to get back there again. I was in the hunt going into the first part of July but I really hadn't done enough to be able to take it easy at all. I'd been battling some injuries; it felt like my knees were about wore out and it was frustrating because it was affecting my riding. I was getting by on broncs but just about the time I really needed to take it to the next level, the knees just weren't there for me.

The turning point that year was when I had Air Wolf at Strathmore. He's one of the best bucking horses there's ever been, and I was looking forward to getting on him. He bucked me off that day and that was a real downer. Maybe he would have got me even if I was healthy, but it sort of symbolized the year I was having.

After that I decided to set my sights on the Canadian Finals, and that was a battle too. Going into August I didn't have a spot clinched by any means, but I was feeling better both physically and mentally. For the two or three weeks just prior to the rodeo at Armstrong, British Columbia, I was riding better than I had all year.

A lot has been made about how that was going to be my last year and one of my last bronc rides. That sounds pretty dramatic in the newspaper but the truth is that could have been said about any of the two or three years before '95. I'd been at it a long time and I'd been thinking on and off about calling it quits for two or three seasons. I suppose I was thinking about retiring a little more seriously that year, mostly because of the way the season had gone. One thing was certain, I'd made up my mind to get both knees scoped at the end of the Canadian Finals to see what I had left.

But I certainly hadn't made a commitment to quit. If I'd suddenly got hot and felt good and been winning a bunch, I probably would have started out the next year the same way I had the previous few — with a see-what-happens attitude. And if I'd won the Canadian championship I would have had a bye into the $50,000 round at Calgary the next year. I wouldn't have walked away from that for darn sure.

Cheryl and I had gone out to Armstrong a day early and really enjoyed the trip through the mountains. It was the first time I'd ever really taken the time to just enjoy the drive. It was a beautiful day and we had a great time. It's funny but I remember all the details of that day. It was almost like there was something inside me that knew this was my last hurrah and I was going to go through some hell for the next while.

The horse I'd drawn that night was named Blue Boy. I'd had him earlier that season at Morris. I'd tried something a little different on him that time. He was a nervous horse in the chute, not mean, he just wanted out of there, and my tactic at Morris was to try to surprise him. I wanted to kind of sneak out of there before he really knew what was going on. But it didn't work. He reared down the chute, and I didn't get a very good go at him. I was behind him the first few jumps and it took me half the ride to catch up.

At Armstrong, I figured I could win some money on him even though it hadn't gone well in Morris. I decided I'd take more time and try to get him standing just right so I could have an honest shot with him. I might have taken too long on him. I knew he was anticipating the gate and getting more and more nervous. Looking back at it, I think he'd just had enough and freaked out a little bit.

He reared back and drove me into the back of the chute. That hurt some but if it had ended there I'd have been all right. But when he came back down, he lost his footing a little bit. As he was trying to regain his balance, he more or less threw himself trying to get his back feet back under himself and he slammed me again. That's when the damage was done. I remember the saddle coming back and that usually spells trouble. It all happened real fast; it was whack-whack and the next thing I knew I was on the ground.

I knew right away I was hurt, but I'd been hurt before and didn't really think this was any big deal. I thought maybe I had the wind knocked out of me or maybe broke some ribs. I'd been there and done that enough times that I was sure I'd be able to get up in a few minutes and shake it off. I guess as cowboys that's the way we're programmed to think.

It wasn't very long before there were people gathered around to help. At first I was just doing my own check to see what was wrong. But I had a really strange sensation. I was lying on my back and it felt as if my feet were straight up in the air. I thought to myself, "I wonder why somebody doesn't put my feet down."

But when I looked, I couldn't see my feet where I thought they should be.

I knew something wasn't right. The medics were asking me if I could feel this or that but I still wasn't thinking that something terrible had happened. *In a minute from now or maybe ten minutes I'll be fine.*

On the way to the hospital in Vernon, they had me hooked up to an IV. I asked if it was steroids because I'd read they get the steroids going right away to reduce the swelling around the spine. They told me it was. When I got to the hospital, nobody was saying much, probably because they didn't know much at that point. But a lot of my cowboy friends were coming by to see me, and the look on their faces told me quite a bit.

After a few hours they airlifted me to Vancouver. They gave me a choice of going either to Calgary or Vancouver. I would have preferred Calgary, but even then I was thinking like a pilot. With my flying background, I knew the mountains between us and Vancouver weren't as rugged. It was the middle of the night when we got airborne for Vancouver.

There was a fair amount going on in that airplane. They had me on oxygen and were monitoring everything real close. At the time I was thinking all the attention wasn't really necessary. Later I realized there's a bunch of other things that can go wrong, and they were doing all they could to make sure nothing did. Cheryl was with me. We were expecting, and actually I was thinking more about her and what she must be going through being seven months pregnant and worrying about me. I was concerned that the stress she was feeling might bring the baby on too soon.

Cheryl was fantastic throughout the whole thing. I'm sure there was stuff she handled that I don't know about to this day. There's all the paperwork that I never even saw and all the people and calls to deal with. It's hard enough to be seven months pregnant under normal circumstances and then throw in what she had to go through with me. That's something I've thought about a lot.

We got to Vancouver and did the hospital thing for the rest of that night and the next day. Tuesday morning when the doctor came in I asked him to be straight with me and he was. What he told me hasn't changed one bit since he told it to me. I had a broken sternum, broken ribs and a broken vertebra, I think it was the ninth, but it was a severe bruise of the spinal cord that really did the damage. He lifted up a can of Copenhagen I had there and dropped it on the table from about four inches up. He explained that that's all it takes if the blow hits in just the wrong spot.

Actually that can of Copenhagen was a hot topic of conversation in the hospital. I don't think too many people there had ever seen snuff before. Some of the nurses thought it was shoe polish. I told them it was a miracle drug.

I'm not going to say it isn't a big shock when a doctor says you'll never walk again. It was like the worst bad dream I'd ever had. But it still hadn't really hit home. I kept thinking, "I'll beat this or something will change tomorrow or next week."

They did some surgery on me to stabilize things and inserted a couple of rods in my back. A few days later they got me sitting up and I got a major surprise right then. I found out I had no balance left. I toppled over like a chopped-down tree. That was weird, and I think it was then that I realized just how big a deal this whole thing was. I was going to have to learn all over again how to do even simple things like sitting up.

What I came to dread most was the pin. You'd think with all the medical technology that's out there, somebody would have come up with a better way to test for feeling. I'd been getting jabbed right from the start — first by ambulance guys, then in Vernon hospital, on the plane and now in Vancouver. It seemed like everybody wearing a white coat would eventually show up in my room with pin in hand. It's okay when they're jabbing the parts where there is no feeling, but when they hit a spot where there is feeling, which they do fairly regularly, it gives a fair stab. The most sensitive area was right along the line where the spinal system is shut off. When they stuck that pin in there, I got a jolt.

I could never figure out why one guy didn't read the other guy's chart, but they never did that. Each doctor had his own pin and was going to do his own jabbing. After a while I began to feel like a human pin cushion.

I didn't really have a game plan for how I was going to deal with things other than just to take things a day at a time. I know that's a cliché but in a deal like this it's true. I had a tremendous amount on my plate every day in terms of new situations to deal with and things to learn and re-learn. I tried to concentrate on that as much as possible. I didn't have time to get angry or think, "Why me?" A lot of people were telling me what a great attitude I had but I was just trying to get through each day. I think it would have been a lot worse if I'd spent all my time thinking and worrying about what the next ten or twenty years were going to be like. And anybody who has spent any time in a hospital knows that no matter how badly off you are, there's always somebody down the hall who's in worse shape.

One of my first visitors was Rick Hansen. I'd always admired what he had done when he toured the world, and I was really glad to meet him. He came up every now and then to visit the guys on the ward, and we spent an hour or so together. He just asked me to think about what had worked for me in rodeo and suggested I try to put those same things to work for me now. It was good advice, and I'm honestly convinced that my rodeo training, particularly the mental part of it, is the biggest thing that has helped me through this.

Rick kidded me about how I wouldn't be able to get out of work at home. I'd still be expected to help around the house and look after the kids. I found him to be a real genuine person. But most of all, the way he has lived his life and dealt with his disability is an inspiration. The thing that still amazes me is that if I have to wheel into the wind or up a grade I get a heck of a workout. I can't even imagine wheeling one of those chairs around the circumference of the globe.

Since my injury, I've become very aware of people with similar injuries. I read the paper and follow their stories on TV and so on. Christopher Reeve's injury happened not long before mine, and I remember feeling bad for the guy. But I was like most people who look at things like that as something that happens to other people. And I was pretty naive about what it really means to have that kind of injury. A rodeo friend, Chuck Simonson, had been paralyzed some years before and I had another friend, a guy I'd played hockey with, who got hurt when we were still in high school. I still tell him I don't know how he went through what he did. I'm very fortunate in that there's been a lot of progress in dealing with injuries like mine. It's much better now than it was even fifteen years ago.

There was a lot of emotion around me, and I knew my family was having a real tough time with it. I guess it's times like that when we realize how much people care about us. I received so much mail I couldn't keep up with it, and it was a while before I finally got caught up. What surprised me was how many people I'd never met sent cards and letters. There were phone calls from all over as well. I don't think it's possible to express how much I really appreciated the interest so many people had in how I was doing.

There were fundraisers that really helped out as well. On the one hand, it felt good that so many people were behind me but there was an unreal feel to it as well. As auctioneers, one of the things we do is the various charity functions to help out different organizations and individuals. It certainly never crossed my mind when I was at those charity events that one day people would be putting them on for me. Wrangler brought me into their program as one of their spokespersons even though I hadn't been before. That was a tremendous gesture on their part, and I was really grateful to them for it.

The money people raised for us was a tremendous help. There was a lot of expense in changing everything about our environment, things like modifying the house and vehicle. It would be awful tough to go through all this and have to worry about the financial part of it too. I'm sure there are lots of people in that situation, and I was mighty glad I wasn't.

There was one particularly nice moment for me while I was still in Vancouver. I received word that I'd won the All-Around Championship. I knew the rodeo chapter of my life was over, and it felt good to win one more time an award I'd always really cared about. At least all the agonizing over when to retire was no longer necessary. That decision was made for me.

Eventually I was put into rehab at the Glen Rose Centre in Edmonton. I found out that that's when the real work begins. The whole thing about rehab is they're just getting you ready to go back into the outside world. And that world is a totally new one.

I had to learn everything — how to get dressed and ready in the morning, how to go to the washroom and take care of my body, all the stuff nobody thinks about. Suddenly I was forced to think about those things because nothing was the same as it was before the injury.

I had to learn to listen to my body. I didn't have all the sensors I had before. And it was important, especially for that period of time when my body was in turmoil and trying to adjust to the changes that had happened to it, that I paid attention. I had to realize that when I didn't feel quite right, it meant something was wrong. Before the injury, I was like most people who just shake it off when things aren't quite right. I couldn't do that any more.

I'd set a goal for myself that I wanted to attend the Canadian Finals Rodeo. When it came time, they didn't want to let me out of there but I told them I was going, no matter what. I did go and I think it was good for me. It took me about an hour to get dressed. The medical types told me jeans were out because they could cause pressure sores. But I knew it was time to get back to living my own life, and when I got to the rodeo I was wearing Wranglers and my cowboy hat. It felt so good to be me again.

It was great going to that Finals, seeing old friends and being presented with my All-Around award. As I accepted the award in the Coliseum the last night of the Finals, I had an odd mix of feelings. I'd made my miles in rodeo so I wasn't feeling all that bad about leaving the competition behind, and yet there was a part of me that was wishing that wasn't my last moment in a rodeo arena. I'd actually qualified for the Finals, and there's no doubt I would have loved to be riding there instead of watching.

The hardest thing to deal with was seeing all the people I knew and who had known me in my pre-wheelchair life. It was awkward for me and I think it was really awkward for them. Most people just don't know what to say. Some would stand in front of the wheelchair and just shake their heads. A lot of times I'd have to start the conversation. I'd tell them I'm fine and things are good and then they'd loosen up a little. Kids are the best. They just come up and admire the wheels or they want to know how fast the chair will go. I don't blame the people who have trouble knowing what to say. I used to be the same way when I'd see somebody who was sick or hurt.

I spent a week out of the rehab centre, and it pretty much told me I was ready to be out of there permanently. I think there's a danger in allowing yourself to become institutionalized and it's easy to do. When I was in there, it was convenient; people were looking after me, and I think a person could get used to that way of living if he let himself. I went back there after the Finals, but I was only there for a few days. I'd stolen one of the "Do Not Disturb" signs from the hotel and I hung it on my door at the rehab centre. They let me sleep till nine in the morning my first day back but after that the sign didn't have much effect.

One year later I went back to Armstrong. It was something I wanted to do. Before the rodeo, I wheeled in behind the chute I'd been in, then out front to where I'd hit the ground. I spent about five minutes there, and it brought it all back to me. I wanted to do that so I could deal with it one final time. Later I opened the rodeo and spoke to the crowd. I don't think I said anything special but I wanted the people there to know I was okay. I'd been doing a lot of speaking at graduations and different functions, and I was quite comfortable with talking to crowds about adversity and how I had dealt with it. But certainly going back to Armstrong exactly a year after the accident felt a little strange.

People often comment on the fact that I don't spend a lot of time feeling sorry for myself.

The fact is there isn't a day goes by that I don't feel frustrated. Living like this is a pain, a big pain. I can't physically do the things I used to. I like being around the cattle, and I wish sometimes I could just walk out there and do normal things. The challenge is to find a way to get around the disability and still live as normally as possible. I try to do something new and learn something new every day. I learned to run the garden tractor using a couple of two-by-fours for foot pedals. I ran into the fence a couple of times but eventually I got so I wasn't bad.

One of my goals when I got home was to catch, saddle, bridle, get on and ride a horse. I wanted to do everything from start to finish without any help. With no balance, my style now is the equivalent of riding a horse while sitting on a basketball. But it was something I wanted to do. I'd been home for about a year. I had a box stall set up with a ramp and I had a special customized saddle made, but the most important thing is a quiet horse.

I was sweating pretty good by the time I was able to get myself out of the wheelchair and up into that saddle but I managed to get it done. I only did that once. I still ride from time to time, but now I get a little help. Once I'm in the saddle, I take it pretty easy most of the time but even then things can get a little western. It's a wild-looking scene when I try to get a cow in. If I have to chase her at all, my legs are flopping around and kicking my horse in the belly while I'm jerking on his head and bouncing all over. It isn't real pretty but I can usually get that cow where I want her.

I think the most important thing for me — and this is something I stress when I'm talking to groups — is to limit my frustration to no more than five minutes. That goes back to my rodeo background too. When I made a bad ride, I tried not to let it bother me for too long. I got my pouting over with in a hurry and got on with things. It's the same thing with this. I know I'm going to get down sometimes but if I can keep the down moments to a minimum, it's going to be a lot easier on me and the people around me. For instance, I hate having to tear my chair down every time I get into a vehicle. It's a pain, no doubt about it, but when I think of all the people who can't get into a vehicle at all *or* tear down their own chair, my inconvenience isn't such a big deal after all.

I do believe that with the medical technology we have today there's a chance that one day they'll figure out a way to heal this kind of injury. But at the same time I can't spend my life waiting for that to happen. The reality is that I may spend more of my life in a wheelchair than I did out of one. And if that's the way it is, I'm okay with that.

The biggest thing is to be glad for what I have rather than worrying about what I don't have. I'm still the same guy I was. I can't do all the things I once did but I'm totally self-sufficient. I have a thousand reasons to get up in the morning. I have a terrific family, a good job auctioneering that I really enjoy and I'm still involved in the sport I love.

All in all, I'd say things are pretty darn good.

Rodeo in the New Millennium

The point has already been made that the Y2K world of today's rodeo competitors is a very different one from that of their ancestors. To today's cowboy and cowgirl, the cell phone is as critical a piece of equipment as his bull rope or her barrel-racing saddle. Change is happening as fast in the rodeo world as it is in the world around us and just as in business or engineering or the arts, technology is at the forefront of that change. Yet there are those in rodeo who want things to be the way they were . . . or at least to slow the pace of change. As more and more competition for the entertainment dollar pops up almost daily, rodeo finds itself struggling to hold its place as a spectator sport. Events that feature only bull riding are eroding what was once rodeo's hallowed domain. Rodeo, in its attempts to attract a new breed of fans, is undergoing something of an identity crisis. The sport that was for so long associated with the old west now employs pyrotechnics and even hard rock music in an effort to appeal to a younger fan base. Where do the competitors sit amidst the change that is happening all around them? Where is rodeo heading? Where should it be heading? What's right and what's wrong with a sport that has relied for so long on tradition but (perhaps) needs to change the way it has always done things if it wants to survive?

✳ **M O N I C A** ✳

Rodeo is the sport I love but it's far from perfect. The biggest problem is the money . . . the money that isn't there. The athletes in rodeo aren't being paid in proportion with the effort it takes to be really good at this sport. We're not in the same league as most professional sports and I think we should be, if not equal, at least a lot closer than we are now.

I doubt if there are many people, particularly in Canada, who are rodeoing for the money. In Barrel Racing there are only three or four girls who do really well financially and that goes back again to horse power. There just isn't that much money to go around, and what there is mostly winds up in the pockets of very few people — the ones with talent and real good horses.

On top of that we still have to pay entry fees to compete. If we didn't, the amount of money put up by most committees wouldn't make it worthwhile to even go. There are rodeos where the money from entry fees is more than the prize money. That really irritates me — going to a rodeo and running at our own money. At the All-Star Challenge in Saskatoon and the Canadian Finals Rodeo, we don't have to pay fees and our rooms are complimentary. I sure don't hear anybody complaining about not having to pay fees there.

The money is getting better now. Rodeos like Ponoka, Cloverdale, Strathmore, Calgary and some others have added more money in recent years and they've become really good rodeos for anyone who does well there. Still not many of us are able to rodeo full-time. Since 1993 I've had a day job at Universal Genetics, which is about four minutes from my house. It's a company that acts as a bull stud station, collecting semen and shipping it around the world. My job is mainly secretarial. I don't take a lunch break, which allows me to get off an hour earlier to get home and ride. And they've been great about giving me time off to rodeo. I think quite a few of us owe a lot of our success to understanding bosses and fellow employees.

I believe that if rodeo is going to become a big league sport it has to adopt a tier system. I'd like to see an "A" series and a "B" series with the best contestants and the best stock at the "A" series. There might be only thirty or forty rodeos in the top tier but those rodeos, because they are the best, would attract television and corporate revenue. And they could pay out a heck of a lot more to the competitors than they do now.

Contestants could move up or down the ladder depending on how they were doing. If a barrel racer's horse was hurt, the cowgirl could drop down to the "B" series and regroup. Best of all, if there was a limited number of rodeos that qualified cowboys and cowgirls for the CFR, then we wouldn't have to go to so many little rodeos to try to make the Finals.

And that's another issue. I have a problem with some of the rodeos we call pro. There are rodeos we shouldn't be at. It's plumb ridiculous and in some cases it's dangerous. The problem is that we don't have standards that committees have to meet in order to have a pro rodeo. And that's wrong. I'm not saying that small rodeos are necessarily bad rodeos; in fact, there are some excellent rodeos that aren't very big at all. But there are also some that are terrible. There should be a committee that makes sure every rodeo has met the standards set out to make it a pro rodeo.

Those standards need to apply to all rodeos. I got in plenty of trouble at Edmonton in '99 because it came out in the media that the girls weren't going to run unless the ground was fixed. But we don't work our butts off all year to get to the CFR and fall down the first night. That happened three years in a row. We heard lots of excuses — this guy isn't allowed to drive that machine or the dirt got rained on or snowed on — but the point is after twenty-five years they ought to know how to fix these problems. Good ground is important for all the events, not just barrel racing.

Professional rodeo in Canada is run by a general manager and an elected board made up of competitors, committee people and contractors. One of the difficulties in bringing changes to rodeo is that the people who run the sport don't always look at what's good for the whole sport. They tend to concentrate on their own area and what's good for them personally. The makeup of the board itself is out of whack too. We have two rough stock and two timed-event contestants elected to serve several hundred members; we have two committee members who look after sixty or so rodeo committees and then we have two stock contractor members who serve the interests of maybe twelve contractors. As a result the contractors have a larger say in what goes on in the sport than their numbers should allow. I don't think that's a good thing.

One of the things we need to do in the future is make stars of our rodeo athletes. That isn't happening now. With the exception of Ty Murray and maybe Fred Whitfield, most people, even sports fans, probably couldn't name a rodeo competitor. We can't make stars out of cowboys and cowgirls who are in town for an hour and a half and gone again. Or who compete in the slack with nobody there to see them. I can't imagine the crowd for a big golf tournament showing up to see Tiger Woods and being told that he golfed yesterday when there was no one around. At lots of rodeos the top three or four places are won in the slack. The reason there's slack at all goes back to there being too many competitors at these rodeos. Slack is great for the competitors who want to get to another rodeo that same day, but it sure cheats the fans.

If we can make our stars as recognizable as the stars in other sports, sponsors will pick them up and things can become a lot easier financially for rodeo competitors. Because we *are* athletes. We train, we train our horses, we're as dedicated to what we do as any athlete in any sport. Maybe in the old days, people got into rodeo because it was cool or because they liked the wild life. Cowboys stayed in town after the rodeo and went to the dance and had fun.

Those days are gone. It's so different now that it would really be fun to have one of those old-time cowboys follow us around for a day just to see how we do things. Today's professional rodeo competitors are just that — professional. This is a business and the people who are most successful are the ones who do the best job of looking after business. Just entering a weekend of rodeos and getting to those rodeos in a way that makes sense travel-wise takes planning and organization. My guess is that every rodeo competitor has a cell phone, most have computers and more and more have Web pages. We use the Internet to get to the PRCA and CPRA sites to check schedules, results and standings. We're about as Y2K as anybody out there.

One way to create rodeo stars is to get the sport in front of more people . . . new people. I believe taking rodeo into new markets — mainly the big centres in the east — is really important if we want to grow. If we can get rodeo into the large eastern cities, I think television and new sponsorship will follow. This sport is so exciting and the athletes so incredible that I really believe if we expose rodeo to people on a regular basis they're going to love it.

And they're going to love rodeo's competitors. Because we have no guaranteed wage like a lot of athletes, we compete when we're hurt and when we're sick. I saw Kelly Armstrong and Austin Beasley at a rodeo recently. They were hurrying to catch a plane to head to a Bull Riding back east somewhere. Kelly had the flu and looked just awful. I can't imagine going somewhere and getting on a bull as sick as he was. But that's what they were doing. Austin had to almost carry him to the plane and off they went. I doubt that too many of the millionaire athletes in some of the team sports would have given a thought to competing feeling like that.

I'm often asked how women are treated in rodeo. I think for the most part, women in rodeo are treated as equals by the majority of the men. There are exceptions as in every part of society, but most people in our sport are aware of how much effort it takes to be a barrel racer. It might surprise some people but the bull riders are the best in terms of treating us as equals. Maybe it's because they tend to be the younger guys, but I also think their attitude is whatever works well for the sport is fine with them.

I sometimes think we should have gone with the bull riders when a number of them went on their own. If we'd made the move with them when they went independent, I think we'd be a lot further ahead. It would have been a perfect match — the age-old concept of beauty and the beast — and I think the fans would have really liked the combination.

Despite the flaws — not in rodeo, but in the running of rodeo — I'm hoping we're going to turn the corner one day soon and that this sport will finally gain the financial status and the respect it deserves. And I think we will. A long-range planning committee has been formed and I like the direction it is taking.

Wouldn't you know it...just as things are finally about to improve in the sport, I'm getting older and won't be going all that much longer. That's okay though. My kids and their kids will be part of a sport that is not only the most fun there is but can work economically as well.

✳ KELLY ✳

I'm concerned about rodeo. I'm sure there are going to be substantial advances on the technology side of how we rodeo with computers, the Internet, more advanced cell phones and the like but that's not the problem. The problem is that the economics of rodeo just isn't keeping up with the cost of going down the road. I'd be surprised if more than the top five people in any event are making money. In 1997 I filed taxes with a gross income of $207,000. Not bad except that it cost me over $150,000 to make that money. What other professional athlete spends three dollars to make four?

The real difficulty is in finding new money for the sport. I'm sure that every potential corporate sponsor in North America has been hit up by the various sports, charities and arts groups to the point that there just isn't a lot of money out there. When I look at the roster of major sponsors in pro rodeo in Canada and the United States, I don't see many new sponsorship dollars flowing in. It's the same companies that have been there all along — and thank God for Wrangler and Dodge and the beer companies and Justin Boots in the States and Brahma and Skoal in Canada and a few others — but where's the new money?

To me the number one limiting factor in rodeo today is the lack of television exposure. If I'm a sponsor, I'm looking at whether to spend my money on baseball, football, hockey, golf or rodeo. Guess which one I'm eliminating first . . . and the reason is that rodeo, with a few exceptions, isn't on nationwide TV. Yes, the NFR and CFR are on TV and so are the new Wrangler Series in the States, which are carried on TNN and ESPN. Those are good moves, but our TV exposure is still a drop in the bucket compared to other major league sports.

I can't say I'm optimistic about the people who run rodeo going out and making the improvements the sport needs in order to really move into the big leagues. They could do it if they wanted to, no doubt about it; just look at the PBR and what it has accomplished. People laughed when the PBR was founded. They said a bunch of dumb bull riders could never pull it off. Well, guess what — those bull riders weren't so dumb after all. They showed what people with good ideas and the will to make something work can do. I just hope rodeo is looking at the success of the PBR and learning something. You can't have a major league sport with minor league money. Rodeo isn't going to disappear, it's just that it will never be at a higher level than it is right now unless the economics of competing get a whole lot better.

There have been some positive things happening in the sport and that's good. One of the areas where I have seen real advances is in the area of protective equipment. There's no doubt that the introduction of the vest has cut down on injuries and protects bull riders. The vest is similar to the bulletproof vest the police wear. It's designed to spread the shock over a greater area when a bull does step on a guy. It's the best thing to come along since I've been around rodeo.

What we need next is protective headgear that works and is comfortable. It has to be lightweight but still able to withstand the blow a bull can apply to it. If we can come up with headgear that is as effective as the vest, we can pretty well eliminate fatalities from bull riding. The upper body and the head are the two areas where the serious injuries occur, and if we can protect them, riding bulls will be a lot safer than it has been.

Another positive is the aggressive marketing of rodeo that is starting to happen in the United States. It's a long way from where it needs to be but the PRCA is at least making an attempt. Now there needs to be a lot more of that kind of thinking. In Canada I would say the situation is worse. Good rodeos are dropping by the wayside, and the money going into cowboys' pockets is still a long way from what it should be. I believe we're at the point where we need new and dynamic ideas to make things better. And we need them now.

As for the production of the rodeos themselves, that's another area that needs big-time attention. I go to some of these three-and-a-half-hour deals and see fans looking bored as hell in the stands while the committees are thinking they're doing a wonderful job because they're giving people lots of rodeo. I think quality is much more important than quantity when it comes to putting on any kind of entertainment.

I hear people say that one of the big changes we're facing in the future is bulls that will be almost impossible to ride. I honestly don't think it's possible for bulls to get ranker than they are now. I think bulls that were considered rank twenty years ago would still be considered rank today. They'd still get their share of buckoffs in the year 2000. And I think today's bulls would buck off the cowboys of 2025.

What I think we will see is more of those really tough bulls. With the sophisticated breeding programs that are out there now, every stock contractor will have more and more of the top-end bulls and fewer and fewer of the middle-of-the-road, filler-type bulls. Breeding bucking bulls is as well thought out — at least by a number of people in this business — as any thoroughbred or quarter horse breeding programs.

In my own program I spend a lot of time trying to work out the best match based on size, temperament and especially the bucking style of the bull compared to the bucking style of the cow's father. If the bull that sired that cow didn't kick that much, then I'll breed the cow to a bull that really kicks. I'm always looking for ways to increase the percentage of good ones I'm producing. It's a numbers game. These contractors need potloads of good bulls. And some of them have no interest in the breeding side of the business. They prefer to buy bulls. As long as when that gate opens, that bull is bucking and spinning they don't much care who his daddy was or what his momma was like. That opens the door for someone like me. I just love to be able to trace the bloodlines of my young bulls back several generations. That's what interests me. As a result, the old fifty per cent buckers quota is a thing of the past. There are breeding programs out there with buck ratios of better than ninety per cent.

The other person who benefits from the increase in the numbers of quality bulls is the competitor. More really good bulls means equal opportunity to win and that evens out the playing field. That's what the bull rider wants. I look at the NFR, and the one area I think really sucks about that rodeo is the so-called eliminator pen. A lot of those bulls are hunks of crap that guys wouldn't win anything on if they did ride them. And those bulls are bucked twice in the ten days, which I guess looks good to the media and people who don't know any better. They can say, "Gee, isn't it neat that only one guy rode tonight? Weren't those great bulls?"

Well, they weren't great bulls. As a matter of fact, a lot of 90-point bulls get left at home so the contractors can bring their eliminators. And they are eliminators — for about three seconds. That's when they get most of the guys. If a cowboy gets past that point in the ride, a lot of those bulls want to quit so bad, those contractors' heads would be shaking. People bash the bull riders at the NFR but the fact is they aren't being given an opportunity to show their talent.

Unlike here in Canada where the cowboys vote on the bulls that go to the CFR with a pretty good knowledge of the stock, in the United States there are so many contractors and so many bulls that it's impossible to really know what we're voting for. When I went to the NFR in '97, I got on a bull that not only had I never heard of, I hadn't even heard of the stock contractor who owned him.

Down there we look at a judge's card and see a bull that was marked 24 points (out of a possible 25) and we think, "Hey, this sucker must be good." But a lot of those 24s were for rides that lasted one and a half seconds. We vote based on that judge's card and bingo, another eliminator goes to the National Finals.

I never thought I'd say this but the day could come when I limit myself to PBR events and not go to rodeos at all. If that happens, it will be strictly economics. When I look at the top fifteen bull riders in the PRCA Bull Riding standings I see that a lot of great cowboys who were in those standings in other years aren't there now. The reason is that they aren't competing at rodeos anymore; they've gone to the PBR. I really don't want to leave traditional rodeo behind — it's where my roots are — but I have to go where the money is. I'm not going to be doing this forever; I have to make it now for myself and my family. I guess the bottom line is that there's tremendous potential for rodeo to grow but I'm not getting my hopes up.

For the moment though I'll be staying mainly with rodeo. I'll work a few PBR events but I have some unfinished business as far as rodeo is concerned. Qualifying for the NFR in 1998 and then not being able to go because of my knee injury left a big hole in my career that I want to fill. To do that I have to qualify again for the NFR. But just getting there won't be enough. I want to be able to walk out of there feeling I did the best I can do. I don't have to win a world championship but I'd like to be leaving Las Vegas knowing I had as good a Finals as I'm capable of.

* DUANE *

I know that probably every generation has thought rodeo was at a crossroads but I really do believe that's the case today. I think we're on the bottom floor with a long way to go to get where we need to be. The good news is we can get there, but I think the changes that have to come to rodeo are going to be hard on some guys.

We're at a point where someone just saying he's a professional cowboy isn't good enough. There's only going to be room for maybe the top twenty people in each event. That's the only way we're going to get television really involved and TV is the most important thing.

There will always be a place for the weekend cowboy but that place isn't going to be at the top professional rodeos. On the PGA Tour, the local club pro golfer doesn't play in the same events as Tiger Woods. We've got to get to that point in rodeo if we really want to be professional and make household names out of our top guns. And it's started already. Rodeos like Calgary and Houston have limited entries and qualification rules. More rodeos are wanting to go that way. The problem right now is that the cowboys aren't being compensated for the fact that some people are being weeded out. It's great for the contractors who don't have to bring as much stock but it has to be great for the contestants too.

The PBR has taken the lead with the way they're doing things, and we have to do something similar. I really admire what the bull riders have accomplished. They're creating more fans all the time, and that has to be good for rodeo too. If those guys can do what they've done, I wonder what some of our big rodeo committees that have just used the cowboy for a century could do if they only wanted to. The PBR does have the luxury of running its own show. They set the rules, say this is how we're doing it and that's the end of the discussion. In rodeo there are so many elements wanting to run things their own way that we may have a lot more trouble moving ahead.

In the PBR the Bud Light Cup is for the cream of the bull riders; in addition, they have a second tour for guys to prove themselves and earn the right to be in the big tour. Rodeo has to go the same way with the best competitors and the best stock at the best rodeos. It would be like taking the CFR or the NFR on the road. That's how we'll attract both TV and corporate dollars. The new PRCA commissioner is trying to move in that direction, and he's taking some heat for it but I think he's on the right track.

We'll have to step on some toes to get to the level we need to be at but we either do that or go all the way back to the way things were in the fifties. Everybody can just pack a picnic lunch and go to the rodeo to hang out and have a good time. The bottom line is money, and we have to see more of it in rodeo. We've got guys laying their lives on the line, particularly in the Bull Riding, and the compensation has to be there.

I think people need to be aware that rodeo is part of our heritage. We're still a young nation and this is a big part of who we are, especially in the west. As people get sicker and sicker of the ridiculous salaries of the other major sports, rodeo is going to have more and more appeal because it really is the last sport where people do it for the love of the game. When I talk about more money for the cowboys and cowgirls in rodeo, I'm not talking about the kind of money basketball players or baseball players are getting. I'm just talking about a reasonable living for people who are professional athletes.

Rodeo is a hard sport to learn, and sometimes we don't do a good enough job of making rodeo fan-friendly so that newcomers to the sport can understand everything that's going on. But once people do get on the inside of the sport, it seems like they're hooked. And I think there are things we can do to make our sport more understandable.

I look at the spur-out rule as an example. I'm not one who thinks we should get rid of it — but I think it should be modified at a rodeo like the NFR where there are so many go-rounds. Instead of a bareback rider or bronc rider getting zero for not having his heels in front of the horse's shoulders that first jump out of the gate, I'm an advocate of making it a penalty of so many points, maybe five per side — like the barrier penalty in the roping events and steer wrestling. Ropers and doggers don't get a no-time for breaking a barrier; a barrel racer doesn't get a no-time for knocking over a barrel.

Making a missed spur out a penalty rather than a no score would do two things. It would be less of a negative for the fans who probably don't see the guy miss spurring the horse out a lot of the time. It's tough when they're getting all excited about what they think is an exceptional ride — and it is — but the rider gets zero. The other benefit would be rough stock cowboys wouldn't necessarily be out of the average and the championship hunt based on a thrown flag.

There's an art to spurring out a horse. There are horses that are really hard to get a good spur out on. For the bronc rider to keep his feet out there on those tough horses, he really has to be on his rein to keep his butt down in the saddle. There's a lot going on to make it work, and I admire a guy like Rod Hay who can spur out a bad horse and look good doing it.

Another area that's a tough sell for rodeo is the Calf Roping and I think it's something we need to do something about. I've said for years that we should be putting protective collars on the calves. They've got wraps for the horns in Team Roping so it's not like we *can't* do something. It'll be a lot more work to put the collars on the calves and then get them accustomed to it but it would certainly be a step in the right direction. I think the biggest thing collars would do is eliminate the perception that the calves are being hurt. I don't honestly believe that roping these calves as few times as we do *does* hurt them, but I also understand that it *looks* like we could be hurting them. Perception is everything. I think it's important that we recognize the fans' concern and do something to improve the image of that part of our sport.

The resistance will come from the ropers themselves because collars might introduce another variable into the mix. There may be calves that run out there bucking and shaking their heads because of the collars and I know that would be a concern. And there will be more cost so right away there's the question of who is going to pay. But I believe it has to happen for the good of the sport. If we do nothing, I can see a big outcry and we could lose Calf Roping altogether. I'd certainly be willing to try the collars at Innisfail on an experimental basis to get the ball rolling.

There are problems on the production side of rodeo. And part of the problem is that we can't set one standard for rodeos. There are rodeos that are day-long picnics and no one would want them any other way. The rodeo in Hand Hills, Alberta, for example, runs all day and then starts up again after supper. It wouldn't be fair to compare a rodeo like that to the Calgary Stampede but in Hand Hills, it works. It's what the people want and it's a great event, kind of a throwback to a hundred years ago. I'm not sure I'd include it in those elite rodeos I referred to but there darn sure is a place somewhere in the rodeo world for a Hand Hills.

In the bigger centres we have to run the thing off in a little over two hours like a movie and get those people out of there to do whatever they're planning to do with the rest of their night. The production in those places has to be smooth, high-class and crisp. We need to be taking a page from the CFR and NFR and the way those rodeos are produced. Somebody goes for popcorn in Edmonton or Las Vegas and they're going to miss something. The people who produce those rodeos are always striving to make them better. If every rodeo in North America did that, it would help immensely.

When that doesn't happen, everybody is to blame. Committees are a part of it but they're only one part; certainly the stock contractors have to be interested in more than just getting paid and getting out of town, and the competitors can play a part too. There again when television becomes more involved it's going to force some changes on those old traditionalists who like to say this is the way we've always done it and this is the way we're going to continue doing it.

The thing that makes me feel good is that I think we'll get there. It's going to be a struggle and there are going to be people who will fight the changes all the way — there always are. But we *will* get there. We have to.

Life After Rodeo

Like athletes in every sport, the rodeo competitor is eventually

faced with the cold reality of the end of a career and what comes

after. For most involved in the sport of rodeo, that moment comes

at a relatively young age. And with it comes the question: what

now? What does a person do whose energy, thought, ambition, in

fact, whose reason for being for the past ten (or fifteen or twenty)

years has been rodeo? It's over, time to move on. So easy to say,

so difficult to do. For two of our competitors, Kelly and Monica,

they can only speculate about what life after rodeo holds in store

for them. Duane, on the other hand, because of the injury that

forced his premature retirement, has been dealing with the issue

since August of 1995.

✳ **MONICA** ✳

When the competitive part of my career is over, I know that won't be the end of my life in rodeo. I'll continue to live the sport through Randa and Riley and then their kids after that. As for me I'll always work with horses. I'd love to make horses for kids to rodeo on. I think it would be really satisfying to see kids competing in junior rodeos and in high school rodeos on horses I had trained. When Bob retires from teaching, we'll take the horse trailer and some horses and head south to Arizona or somewhere for the winter. I'm looking forward to that because I enjoy working with young horses and it will be nice to finally have time to do some of that.

There's an association called the Canadian Senior Professional Rodeo Association. It's for contestants who want to keep going after their pro careers are over. It used to be called Old-timers Rodeo but I can see why they wanted to change the name. I'm not ready for that kind of rodeo yet. Those people are having too much fun. They go to a rodeo, visit with their friends and stay for the whole weekend. That's really neat but I can't sit still for that long. Down the road I could see myself heading off to those rodeos, especially if Bob got back into competing. But he's too busy right now, and there are still some things I want to do in professional rodeo so the Senior Pro circuit is a ways off yet.

Though there are all those things I might be doing if I wasn't so involved in rodeo, I really don't feel like I've missed out on a lot. Rodeo has been so much more than just a sport. It's been our hobby, our social life, our fitness program and, most of all, our family time.

I'm not sure what it's going to take to make me quit. I suppose if I wasn't competitive any more, I'd get out. I don't think I could just go to rodeos and donate my fees for other people to win. There are people who do that but I won't be one of them.

If I ever do decide to retire or even back off on my rodeo schedule, there are a thousand things I'd like to do. The busyness of our lives means that rodeo people are often excluded — or we exclude ourselves — from our community. This sport seems to consume us. Certainly it consumes our time. We often miss out on a lot of other things because there just isn't time for them. I'd love to take some classes, learn how to make stained glass windows, that kind of thing, and I'd love to have more time to work with the kids in the community. I feel bad too that I don't get to church more than I do. I was raised Roman Catholic but unfortunately that's one of the things in my life that's been put on hold.

Politics has always interested me, although I don't think I'd ever get involved beyond voting and following what's going on through the newspapers and television. I'm a Liberal, always have been. I come from a Liberal family and I was a big Trudeau fan. I'm probably not typical of rodeo people. My guess is that most of them would lean toward the Alliance Party, although I can't say for sure because one thing we don't talk about on the road is politics. We'll get into religious discussions and we'll talk about what's wrong with the world, but party politics just isn't a subject we get into.

My family is very important to me. Bob teaches at a high school nearby, and he judges rodeos and provides timed event cattle at some. My mom lives in the house next door, right across the yard. Bob's dad, Ted, and Maxine come over a lot. We play a lot of cards, which probably goes back to our life on the ranch when there wasn't a lot to do at night. We played a lot of cards then and still do.

I can count on the fingers of one hand the number of times Bob and I go out in a year. There just doesn't seem to be time for that although once in a while we'll go to a movie on a Tuesday night, which is cheap night.

I love to paint. I work mostly in acrylics and watercolours although I don't do very much of either right now because I'm just too busy with rodeo and my job and my family. In fact Bob took all my paints and gave them to one of his high school students who was really talented but didn't have much money for paints. I think I'll get back to my art later when rodeo and some of the other things we're doing slow down.

I sometimes regret that there isn't time now for some of the other things I'd like to do . . . and have. I suppose if I wasn't rodeoing, we might have a bigger, nicer house and time to wallpaper and have a big garden. With the rodeo schedule we all have, we're lucky if the house gets cleaned and the laundry done. But it's difficult not to be totally committed to succeeding when we have so much invested financially in the truck and trailer and horses — seventeen head in our case — as well as the time we've put in to get to this level. It means setting aside a lot of those other things. I guess I'll just have to make those stained glass windows and have that garden a little later in my life.

Right now I've got good horses and I still love competing. I don't think much about five years from now or ten. I'm content to look forward to tomorrow because tomorrow there's another rodeo to go to.

✳ KELLY ✳

If, for some reason, my rodeo career ended next week, I know exactly what I'd be doing. I'd be a working cowboy. I'd want a little place of my own so I could get up in the morning, saddle up and be on a horse until dark. Then I'd repeat the process the next day . . . and the day after that. I would love a life that allowed me to take my wife or my kids and ride off and check cows every day for the rest of my life. We'd treat that calf or that yearling and take a lot of satisfaction in doing it. And what I'd be coming back to at the end of each day would be a little log cabin and a family I care about and that cares about me.

The first thing I plan to change about my life when my rodeo is over is my stress level. Even though I'm only in my early twenties, I must be the most stressed-out guy I know. And I don't want my life to be that way forever. I talk to the kids I went to high school with. They've got jobs that they work at, then they party on the weekend and spend the week's cheque having fun. And here I am getting grey hair. Sometimes I think, "Damn, I'm way too young for that."

But I realize this is a ten-year deal, at the most, then I'll walk away and be able to do those other things I want to do. At the same time I know that I have to slow down and enjoy the view right now. It's hard to do that with the pace of the life we live in rodeo but that's something I have to do.

I worry about money all the time. No matter how good I'm doing I'm always worried about the financial side of things. When I'm driving down the road, it's what I think about a lot of the time. I realize that we live in a world of high finance but for me it's also high stress.

I had a goal to pay my place off in five years. I'm a believer in that old saying "Don't buy it if you can't afford it." I knew I could afford to buy my farm in Big Valley but I still didn't like carrying that debt. I've calculated what it costs me per day to run my farm loan. It costs me $26 a day in interest. I spend a lot of time thinking about all the things I could do with that twenty-six bucks.

I realized that I could actually speed things up and pay it off quicker but to do it I'd have had to trade off seven of my bulls. I didn't feel that all seven were ready to trade right at that time. I wanted to keep them that one more year to make sure they'd be ready for the people who bought them. So there I was worrying about money again.

Austin has had to sit me down a few times and counsel me to just relax a little. But it's hard for me to let go of my concerns about money. I have a pencil case in my briefcase that I put twenty dollars and ten per cent of my earnings in every day. It's amazing how that adds up. Just the twenty dollars a day adds up to $7,300 in a year. And if I can have another $200,000 year I'll have that place paid off well ahead of my five-year goal.

It's not like I've ever been in a money pinch — it's just that it worries me to death to owe somebody money. The truth is, except for using the money from Ponoka that one time, the money I make rodeoing doesn't have to go toward paying off my land. I've got beef cows and rodeo bulls that are worth more than enough. And I've made my payments on time, every time. But damn, I'd like to own it outright.

My number one goal when I walk away from rodeo is to be my own boss. I want independence. That's something I have in my life now, and I would feel robbed if that was ever taken away from me. I work every day at defending that independence because I want so much for it to continue. Sometimes I think I'm a little like a wild horse. They love to run free with nothing holding them back. I'm pretty much the same way.

When my career is over, the first thing I'll want to do something about is the telephone. I'd get rid of the thing. It does nothing but stress me. For sure I won't have one with me when

I'm on that saddle horse checking cows. In fact, I'd like to get away from technology altogether. I've already started making some moves in that direction. This fall I'm planning to buy a team of horses from [bull rider] Jason Finkbeiner's dad. And I'll do my chores with those horses the way it was done in the old days. I guess that sounds funny coming from someone my age who wasn't around in the old days but that's what I want most of all — a simple way of life.

I could see myself becoming awful close to a hermit. I wouldn't even go to town much other than to get supplies and have the odd cup of coffee with my friends. One of the things I'm very sure about — and maybe I'm different from some guys about this — is that I don't want or need to be in the limelight after this is all over. Right now, though, I love it when I get to a rodeo and a kid asks for an autograph. Sometimes I'll see that kid later and he remembers me and wants another autograph to go with the first one. Those are special moments for me.

Competing at rodeos is one phase of my life, and even though it's been the most important thing to me for as long as I can remember, when it's over, it's over. That doesn't mean I'll walk away from rodeo completely. I might be able to take myself out of rodeo but nothing will ever take rodeo out of me. I'll always be playing around with bulls and I'll get to the odd rodeo to swap lies with my rodeo friends.

As for my kids, they're going to grow up around rodeo. But if they tell me rodeo isn't their cup of tea, that there's something else they'd like to do, I know I'll be fine with that as long as they want to do their best at whatever it is they choose to do.

My greatest hope for the future is that I can lead a lifestyle that is more like things used to be: where a handshake meant something, where people's word meant everything, where women were treated like ladies and most of all, where some of those old values make a bit of a comeback. I know that sounds old school, but when I look at the world right now, I think maybe a dose of "old school" wouldn't be so bad.

One of the things that's important to me now and I think will always be important to me is what Tuff Hedeman taught me a long time ago. Tuff's attitude can be summed up in the words "No excuses." That's something I've really come to believe in. The one thing I would hate is for people to say, "Too bad ol' Kelly never gave it his all. He could have been really good if only he'd made the effort."

I want to make the effort. Whether it's riding the rankest bull at the NFR or trying to be a person that cares about people, I want to make the effort.

✳ D U A N E ✳

In 1982 I got my auctioneer's licence. It's always amazed me that there are as many parallels as there are between auctioneering and rodeo. I had to prove myself to earn my stripes in selling just as I did in rodeo. Once a rookie auctioneer has shown he can sell old peed-on mattresses and stuff, he graduates to slaughter cows and eventually to the bigger livestock sales. And I can understand that. We have to prove ourselves in every aspect of life.

One of the surprising similarities between selling and rodeo is that there's pressure on an auctioneer, sometimes big pressure. When I'm selling somebody's calves, that sale represents a good part of that family's income for the year. They need the auctioneer to get the best dollar possible, and the ability to do that comes with experience. So there is pressure, but, on the other hand, the feeling

I get after a sale has gone really well and the seller is happy with the price he got and the buyer is happy with the cows or calves he now owns is about as close to that rodeo feeling as I can get.

I've got some cattle of my own around the place too. I have a little cow-calf herd at home and a few yearlings at another place. I've always loved the cattle business, and I still enjoy getting out there on the trike and checking those cows at calving time.

But rodeo isn't totally gone from my life. And I don't think it ever will be. Everybody says it, I know, but I want to give something back to a sport that gave a lot to me. I'm the Saddle Bronc Riding director on the CPRA Board of Directors, and I'm a member of the Judging Commission. I enjoy the give-and-take of being involved in governing the sport although it's very different from being a competitor. Sometimes I feel kind of out of the loop. I enjoyed going into the dressing room and getting ready to ride. I liked being one of the guys and that's something I do miss. I've talked to other athletes and read about some and they all say that's the part they miss — just being there and being a part of the thing.

The other thing is the adrenaline rush. I loved that part of competing. It started about the time I started my preparation that went into every ride at every rodeo. After thirteen years I had my routine I liked to follow. There was a kind of pre-game warm-up I went through that included everything from eating to getting my equipment ready. I liked the mental part of getting myself up for the ride, although I have to say that as the years went on it became harder and harder to do that. It was still easy at the Canadian Finals but it was tougher at some little rodeo out on the prairie in the rain. That's where I found I had to dig deep to get myself ready to make that ride.

I certainly don't miss the miles; in fact, as I look back on it I can't imagine how I did it. Now just going to Calgary for the day seems like a big adventure. I still get to a fair number of rodeos with Cheryl and her barrel racing. And I think it's important for directors to get out there and see what's going on so we can be knowledgeable in the decisions we make.

The other aspect of my rodeo involvement that I think will go on for a long time is right here with the Innisfail Rodeo. It started up back in 1960 and it's come a long way. Once I got my card and started rodeoing professionally, it seemed like Dad really wanted to make Innisfail one of the top rodeos. And it is. It's very much a cowboys' rodeo. We want to do everything we can, including getting the prize money up there to make this an event that cowboys and cowgirls look forward to coming to. We get all the stock contractors in here with their best horses and bulls so guys have a chance to win. And if they do win, the money's good. Anything we make goes either right into cowboys' pockets or toward improvements for the next rodeo there. We're not a service club trying to raise money to build a parking lot somewhere.

The Bronc Riding is pretty special here at Innisfail. With our family history, we decided a while back to put up even more money in the Bronc Riding and make it like a match. Our bottom line is we want the rodeo contestants to feel important and glad they came to the Innisfail Rodeo.

One of the things I'm doing now that I didn't do enough of earlier in my life is being a part of my daughter's growing up. I always made a point of trying to spend as much time with the girls as I could but it was tough with a hectic rodeo schedule to be there as much as I wanted to be. Now that I'm no longer competing and on the road as much, I'm really enjoying Sydney's figure skating and all the things that she's involved in. Most of all I just get a kick out of watching her grow up and getting to be a part of that.

There's something else that has become important in my life since my accident. I get requests from time to time to visit with people who have injuries similar to mine. I'm always happy to do that. I know how much it meant to me when Rick Hansen came by to see me. The thing I always try to tell people who are struggling with their injury and paralysis is the same thing I tell everybody. We're still the same people we were. We may not be able to do the same things we used to but we still matter. We matter as much as anybody.

I have no regrets. I got in my full slate of rodeos and I won my share of the ones I hoped I'd win. I'm into the next phase of my life now and I'm enjoying it. There are times when I have to work at it but I am enjoying my life.

I'm carrying with me a whole lot of great memories. The faces of rodeo are changing all the time but years from now there will still be the guys I rode with and against; they'll know who I was and how I rode and I believe will respect me for the cowboy I was in the same way that I'll respect them. I learned a lot from my uncle Ivan, too. When his career was over there were still an awful lot of people who really respected him, both in and out of the arena.

I'd like to be thought of in the same way, as a guy who tried his butt off and who was respected and liked in rodeo and in life. That means more to me than all the championships in the world.

GLOSSARY

THE EVENTS

Bareback Riding: With one hand in a bareback rigging — a rawhide, suitcase handle-like handhold — and the other hand free, the contestant attempts to ride for eight seconds. Other than the rider's chaps, spurs and glove, he has no other equipment. The rider spurs by bringing his dull-roweled spurs up the neck of the horse toward the handhold. The rider is marked on his ability to ride and spur while the horse is marked on how it bucks.

Barrel Racing: In an event characterized by horse and rider cooperation, the cowgirl rides a cloverleaf pattern around three barrels. Quick turns and speed between the barrels and on the run home are musts for success in an event where the times are so close and so fast they are measured in hundredths of a second.

Bull Riding: The rider places his gloved hand palm up in the handhold of a flat-woven, heavily resined rope. The tail of the rope is passed around the girth of the bull, pulled tight into the palm of the hand, around the hand and into the palm again. Bull riders are not required to "spur out" the animal nor do they have to spur during the eight-second ride.

Calf Roping: A mounted cowboy chases a calf down the arena, ropes the calf and dismounts from his horse. With a second, smaller rope, called a piggin string, he ties three legs. The calf must stay tied for six seconds after the contestant has re-mounted his horse and slacked the catch rope.

Saddle Bronc Riding: In this classic event of rodeo, the bronc rider sits in a saddle specially designed for this event and holds on to a buck rein. The better riders use that buck rein for balance during the eight-second ride, not to help hold themselves on. He spurs in a sweeping, front-to-back arc from the horse's shoulders to the back of the saddle.

Steer Riding: In professional rodeo, boys fourteen years of age and under ride using a bull rope but with the option of using two hands. Like the other riding events, it is an eight-second ride and is judged using essentially the same criteria as the Bull Riding event.

Steer Wrestling: Also known as Bull Dogging. As their horses reach the hard-running steer, the hazer (a mounted helper) keeps the steer moving straight while the steer wrestler (dogger), from the opposite side, begins to transfer his weight from his horse to the steer. His horse runs on past, carrying the cowboy up to the horns and taking his feet out in front of the steer, in position for the cowboy to slow the steer, turn him and take him to the ground.

THE LINGO

Added money: The total prize money in any event is made up of the entry fees paid by the contestants and the purse put up by the rodeo committee. The purse is called the added money.

Average: One of rodeo's misnomers. Contestants in rodeos with more than one go-round are paid off in prize money for the highest score or fastest time in each go-round and for the best total in all the go-rounds. That total or aggregate is referred to in rodeo as the average. The winner of the average is the winner of that event at the rodeo.

Barrier: A rope stretched across the front of the box from which the roper's or steer wrestler's horse comes when the calf or steer is released. The contestant must give the stock a predetermined head start.

Breaking the barrier: If the contestant rides through or breaks the barrier before it is released, a penalty of ten seconds is added to the time.

Eliminator: A bull that is especially difficult to ride. At the Canadian and National Finals Rodeos, one or two nights are designated for the eliminator pen.

Entry fees: The money paid by the contestant before he or she can compete in an event or rodeo. Contestants must pay a separate fee for every event they compete in.

Flank (flank strap): A sheepskin-lined strap with a self-holding buckle passed around the flank of a bronc or bull. The strap may be pulled tight as the animal leaves the chute. In an effort to get rid of the flank strap, the animal bucks higher and harder.

Go-round: That part of the rodeo that is required to allow each contestant to compete on one head of stock. The number of go-rounds at a rodeo may vary from one to as many as four or more at the larger rodeos.

Hang up: A bareback rider or bull rider will hang up when he is bucked off away from his hand (for example, a left-handed rider is bucked off to his right) and is unable to let go of the rigging or bull rope. The pickup men (in Bareback Riding) and the bullfighters (in Bull Riding) will come to the aid of the cowboy and try to free his hand. It is one of the most dangerous situations that takes place in the rodeo arena.

Miss out: Also referred to as the "spur-out" or "contact" rule. In both Bareback and Saddle Bronc Riding, the contestant must have his heels in front of the points of the horse's shoulders on the first jump out of the chute. This adds a degree of difficulty to the ride and if the cowboy "misses the horse out," by not having his heels forward on that first jump, he receives no score.

No-time: In a timed event, the contestant receives a no-time if he has not caught or thrown his animal properly. A field judge will indicate a no-time with a wave of a flag.

Pickup man: A mounted cowboy who helps the rider off a bucking horse when the ride is completed. The pickup man then removes the flank strap and escorts the horse out of the arena.